THE IDEALS
Treasury
OF Prayer

THE IDEALS
Treasury
OF *Prayer*

Sweet hour of prayer, sweet hour of prayer,
That calls us from a world of care
And bids us at our Father's throne,
Make all our wants and wishes known.
WILLIAM WALFORD

IDEALS PUBLICATIONS INCORPORATED
NASHVILLE, TENNESSEE
WWW.IDEALSPUBLICATIONS.COM

ISBN 0-8249-4187-X

Published by Ideals Publications Incorporated
535 Metroplex Drive, Suite 250
Nashville, TN 37211

Library of Congress Cataloging-in-Publication Data
Ideals treasury of prayer/ Julie K. Hogan, editor.
      p. cm.
   Includes bibliographical references.
   ISBN 0-8249-4187-X (alk. paper)
   1. prayers. 2. Devotional literature. I. Hogan, Julie, 1949-
   BV245 .I34 2000
   242'.8–dc21   00-020441

10 8 6 4 2 1 3 5 7 9

PUBLISHER, PATRICIA A. PINGRY
BOOK DESIGNER, EVE DEGRIE
BOOK EDITOR, JULIE K. HOGAN
ASSOCIATE EDITOR, THORUNN MCCOY
COPY EDITOR, ELIZABETH KEA
RESEARCH ASSOCIATE, MARY P. DUNN

PHOTOGRAPHY BY CARR CLIFTON

ACKNOWLEDGMENTS:

All possible care has been taken to fully acknowledge the ownership and use of every selection in this book. If any mistakes or omissions have occurred, they will be corrected in subsequent editions, provided notification is sent to the publisher.
BAILLIE, JOHN. "Ninth Day–Morning" and "Twenty-Seventh Day–Evening." Reprinted with the permission of Scribner, a Division of Simon & Schuster from A Diary of Private Prayer by John Baillie. Copyright 1949 by Charles Scribner's Sons; copyright renewed © 1977 by Ian Fowler Baillie. CARMICHAEL, AMY. "Keep All My Children" from Learning of God by Amy Carmichael. "Do Thou for Me," "It Is Not Far to Go," "Think Through Me," "Thy Way Is Perfect," and "Tranquillity" from Toward Jerusalem by Amy Carmichael. Copyright © Dohnavur Fellowship, Publisher Christian Literature Crusade, Fort Washington, PA. CROWELL, GRACE NOLL. "Because of Thy Great Bounty," "A Prayer," and "A Prayer for Inner Strength" from The Eternal Things by Grace Noll Crowell. Copyright © 1965 by Grace Noll Crowell. Reprinted by permission of HarperCollins Publishers. "Courage to Live" from This Golden Summit by Grace Noll Crowell. Copyright © 1937. Reprinted by permission of HarperCollins Publishers. CUMMINGS, E. E. "i thank you God for most this amazing." Copyright 1950, © 1978, 1991 by the Trustees for the E. E. Cummings Trust. Copyright © 1979 by George James Firmage, from Complete Poems : 1904–1962 by E. E. Cummings, edited George J. Firmage. Used by permission of Liveright Publishing Corporation. DICKINSON, EMILY. "Of God we ask one favor." Reprinted by permission of the publishers and the Trustees of Amherst College from The Poems of Emily Dickinson, Raulph W. Franklin, ed., Cambridge, Mass.: The Belknap Press of Harvard University Press, Copyright © 1998 by the President and Fellows of Harvard College. Copyright © 1951, 1955, 1979 by the President and Fellows of Harvard College. ELIOT, T. S. Excerpt from Murder in the Cathedral by T. S. Eliot, copyright 1935 by Harcourt, Inc. and renewed 1963 by T. S. Eliot, reprinted by permission of the publisher. Also reprinted by permission of Faber and Faber Ltd. GRAHAM, BILLY. Excerpt form Till Armageddon by Billy Graham, copyright © 1981, Word Publishing, Nashville, Tennessee. All rights reserved. HOLMES, MARJORIE. "The Unexpected" from I've Got to Talk to Somebody, God by Marjorie Holmes and "Learning to Pray" from How Can I Find You, God? by Marjorie Holmes. Used by permission of the author. MARSHALL, PETER. "Prayer" from Mr. Jones, Meet the Master by Peter Marshall. "December 10, 1947," "Evening Prayer," "For Those Who Serve," "Pastorate Prayer for Healing," and "Teach Us to Pray" from The Prayers of Peter Marshall. Used with the permission of Chosen Books, a division of Baker Book House Company. MERTON, THOMAS. Excerpt from Thoughts in Solitude by Thomas Merton. Copyright © 1956, 1958 by the Abbey of Our Lady of Gethsemani. Renewal copyright © 1986 by the Trustees of the Thomas Merton Legacy Trust. Reprinted by permission of Farrar, Straus, & Giroux, Inc. NIEBUHR, REINHOLD. "Serenity Prayer." Used by permission of the Estate of Reinhold Niebuhr. NOUWEN, HENRI J. Excerpt from A Cry for Mercy by Henri J. M. Nouwen, copyright © 1981 by Henri J. M. Nouwen. Used by permission of Doubleday, a division of Random House, Inc. PEALE, NORMAN VINCENT. Excerpt from A Guide to Confident Living by Norman Vincent Peale. Reprinted with the permission of Simon & Schuster, copyright 1948 by Prentice-Hall, Inc.; copyright renewed © 1976 by Norman Vincent Peale. PROULX, RICHARD. "Where Love and Charity Are Found, God Himself Is There," Copyright © 1975 by GIA Publications, Inc., Chicago, Illinois. All rights reserved. Used with permission. RICE, HELEN STEINER. "My Daily Prayer." Used with permission of The Helen Steiner Rice Foundation, Cincinnati, Ohio, copyright © 1976 The Helen Steiner Rice Foundation. All rights reserved. ROSENBERG, DAVID. "The Hundred Thirty-Third Psalm" from A Poet's Bible by David Rosenberg. Copyright © 1991 by David Rosenberg. Published by Hyperion. SANDLIN, JOHN LEWIS. "For the Family" from A Prayer for Every Meeting by John Lewis Sandlin. Used with the permission of Fleming H. Revell, a division of Baker Book House Company. SCHULLER, ROBERT. "Praying for Guidance" from Tough Minded Faith for Tender Hearted People by Robert Schuller. Used with permission of the author. STANLEY, CHARLES. Excerpt from This Glorious Journey by Charles Stanley. Used by permission of Thomas Nelson Publishers. STOREY, VIOLET ALLEYN. "In a Time of Discouragement" from A Poet Prays by Violet Alleyn Storey. Published by Abingdon Press, 1959. Used by permission. MOTHER TERESA. "The fruit of silence" from Total Surrender by Mother Teresa. Reprinted with permission of New World Library, Novato, CA 94949, www. nwlib.com. "Only a Shadow" from My Life for the Poor. Reprinted by permission of HarperCollins Publishers. TOPPING FRANK. "Praising" from Lord of Life. Used with the permission of Lutterworth Press. Our sincere thanks to the following author whom we unable to locate: Vienna Cobb Anderson for "Prayer for Grandparents."

CONTENTS

PRAISE AND TRUST

CHAPTER ONE

*Our Father
which art in heaven,
Hallowed be thy name . . .*

LEARNING TO PRAY

MARJORIE HOLMES

You know, Lord, how well You know, the years when I didn't pray (or didn't think I prayed). How could I pray to someone whose very existence I doubted? How could I ask for help from a force I spurned?

Yet all the while I was hungering for You, groping to find Your hand as I stumbled in the darkness of my needs . . . . "If I could pray," I thought. "If I could only learn to pray."

But I felt foolish when I tried; I felt phony, insincere. My doubts seemed to rise up like a mockery between us. And You knew my follies and my faults all too well. My tongue was inarticulate—it winced to form the words. My own self-scorn made me impotent, dumb.

I would get up from my fumbling so-called prayers with an empty heart, feeling rejected, turned away. (Was there some secret rubric others had discovered? Some key that would make the heavens open, unlock the special doors?)

I was wrong. In a while, maybe from sheer persistence, something began to happen within me. A sense of being accepted, however unworthy. (No—not merely accepted, welcomed, welcomed home!) And the deep excited stirrings of trust in a power I could not see.

Then I went to the formula you gave in the Sermon on the Mount.

"Our father who art in heaven." How kind that seems. "Hallowed be Thy name." The gentle beginnings of worship . . .

"Thy kingdom come" (within me). "Thy will be done" (take over my life, I'm not doing so well) "on earth as it is in heaven." (I like this earth, I don't know about heaven, but it must be a wonderful place.)

"Give us this day our daily bread" (just enough for today, Lord, enough time and money and strength to get through this one day) . . . "and forgive us our trespasses as we forgive" (are my trespasses blocking the road to You? and my lack of forgiveness for those who've hurt me?).

"Lead us not into temptation" (this I don't understand—you couldn't, you wouldn't—just hang on to me when I am tempted, give me the will not to yield). "Deliver us from evil" (yes, yes, that's what I mean—deliverance).

"For Thine is the power and the glory forever and ever." (It is, it is, it has to be, and the more often I admit it, express it, the more I know it's true!)

So in this way I began to get deliverance, Lord. The deliverance I sought. From self-doubt, which was so deeply enmeshed with my doubts of You.

And to learn the fundamentals of prayer: worship, submission, acceptance, plea, and then more worship to seal it. And I began to know then as I realize now that worship itself is the key. The magic key. Prayer brings You close when we come not merely seeking help, but because we want to be with you.

PRAYER OF PRAISE

But let my soul praise Thee that it may love Thee,
And let it tell Thee Thy mercies that it may praise Thee.
Without ceasing Thy whole creation speaks Thy praise—
The spirit of every man by the words that his mouth directs to Thee,
Animals and lifeless matter by the mouth of those who look upon them.
That so our soul rises out of its mortal weariness unto Thee,
Helped upward by the things Thou hast made
And passing beyond them unto Thee who has wonderfully made them:
And there refreshment is and strength unfailing. Amen.
SAINT AUGUSTINE

Prayer is the beginning of an uprising against the disorder of the world.

KARL BARTH

Bless the LORD, O my soul.
O LORD my God, thou art very great;
Thou art clothed with honour and majesty.

PSALM 104:1

THE HUNDRED FOURTH PSALM

Up, O my soul, and bless the Lord. O God,
My God, how great, how very great art Thou!
Honor and majesty have their abode
With Thee and crown Thy brow.

Thou clothest Thyself with light, as with a robe,
And the high, glorious heavens Thy mighty hand
Doth spread like curtains round about this globe
Of air and sea and land.

The beams of Thy bright chambers Thou dost lay
In the deep waters, which no eye can find;
The clouds Thy chariots are, and Thy pathway
The wings of the swift wind.

In thy celestial, gladsome messages
Dispatched to holy souls sick with desire
And love of Thee, each willing angel is
Thy minister in fire.

Thy arm unmovable forever laid
And founded the firm earth; then with the deep
As with a veil Thou hidst it; Thy floods played
Above the mountains steep.

At Thy rebuke they fled; at the known voice
Of their Lord's thunder they retired apace:

Some up the mountains passed by secret ways,
Some downwards to their place.

O Lord my God, how many and how rare
Are Thy great works! In wisdom hast Thou made
Them all, and this the earth and every blade
Of grass we tread, declare.

Thou sendest Thy spirit forth, and they revive;
The frozen earth's dead face Thou dost renew.
Thus Thou Thy glory through the world dost drive
And to Thy works art true.

Thine eyes behold the earth, and the whole stage
Is moved and trembles; the hills melt and smoke
With Thy least touch: lightnings and winds that rage
At Thy rebuke are broke.

Therefore as long as Thou wilt give me breath
I will in songs to Thy great name employ
That gift of Thine, and to my day of death
Thou shalt be all my joy.

I'll spice my thoughts with Thee, and from Thy word
Gather true comforts; but the wicked liver
Shall be consumed. O my soul, bless Thy Lord!
Yea, bless thou Him forever!
HENRY VAUGHAN

WE PRAISE THEE, O GOD

T. S. ELIOT

We praise Thee, O God, for Thy glory displayed in all
the creatures of the earth,
In the snow, in the rain, in the wind, in the storm; in all of Thy creatures,
both the hunters and the hunted.
For all things exist only as seen by Thee, only as known by Thee, all things exist
Only in Thy light, and Thy glory is declared even in that which denies Thee;
the darkness declares the glory of light.
Those who deny Thee could not deny, if Thou didst not exist;
and their denial is never complete, for if it were so, they would not exist.
They affirm Thee in living; all things affirm Thee in living; the bird in the air,
both the hawk and the finch; the beast on the earth,
both the wolf and the lamb; the worm in the soil and the worm in the belly.
Therefore man, whom Thou hast made to be conscious of Thee,
must consciously praise Thee, in thought and in word and in deed.
Even with the hand to the broom, the back bent in laying the fire,
the knee bent in cleaning the hearth, we, the scrubbers and sweepers
of Canterbury,
The back bent under toil, the knee bent under sin, the hands to the face
under fear, the head bent under grief,
Even in us the voices of seasons, the snuffle of winter, the song of spring,
the drone of summer, the voices of beasts and of birds, praise Thee.
We thank Thee for Thy mercies of blood, for Thy redemption by blood.
For the blood of Thy martyrs and saints
Shall enrich the earth, shall create the holy places.
For wherever a saint has dwelt, wherever a martyr has given
his blood for the blood of Christ,
There is holy ground, and the sanctity shall not depart from it
Though armies trample over it, though sightseers come with guide-books
looking over it;
From where the western seas gnaw at the coast of Iona,
To the death in the desert, the prayer in forgotten places by the broken
imperial column,
From such ground springs that which forever renews the earth
Though it is forever denied. Therefore, O God, we thank Thee
Who hast given such blessing to Canterbury.
Forgive us, O Lord, we acknowledge ourselves as type of the common man,

Prayer enlarges the heart...

MOTHER TERESA

Of the men and women who shut the door and sit by the fire;
Who fear the blessing of God, the loneliness of the night of God,
   the surrender required, the deprivation inflicted;
Who fear the injustice of men less than the justice of God;
Who fear the hand at the window, the fire in the thatch, the fist in the tavern,
   the push into the canal,
Less than we fear the love of God.
We acknowledge our trespass, our weakness, our fault; we acknowledge
That the sin of the world is upon our heads; that the blood of the martyrs
   and the agony of the saints
Is upon our heads.
Lord, have mercy upon us.
Christ, have mercy upon us.
Lord, have mercy upon us.

OUR FATHER WHICH ART IN HEAVEN, HALLOWED BE THY NAME

No prayer of adoration will ever soar higher than a simple cry: "I love you, God."

LOUIS CASSELS

HOW SWEET THE NAME OF JESUS

How sweet the name of Jesus sounds
In a believer's ear!
It soothes his sorrows, heals his wounds,
And drives away his fear,
And drives away his fear.

It makes the wounded spirit whole
And calms the troubled breast;
'Tis manna to the hungry soul,
And to the weary, rest,
And to the weary, rest.

Dear name! The rock on which I build
My shield and hiding place;
My never-failing treasure, filled
With boundless stores of grace,
With boundless stores of grace.

Jesus, my shepherd, brother, friend,
My prophet, priest, and king,
My lord, my life, my way, my end,
Accept the praise I bring,
Accept the praise I bring.

JOHN NEWTON

WE PRAISE THEE

JOHN LEWIS SANDLIN

Eternal God, our Father, we praise Thee for the light of day. Thou hast given us so many blessings beyond our deserving. Help us to find meaning in all of life.

Bless our family and its interests, that all we do may find the goals Thou hast inspired. Give us grace to fill every hour with "sixty seconds worth of distance run." So may we live this day that our hearts may find new dedication to the service of our fellows.

Inspire us with truth, that we may learn; endow us with insight, that we may see meaning; bless us with health, that we may be useful to Thee. And as the shadows of the evening fall upon us, grant us peace through Him who is the Prince of Peace. Amen.

Be still, and know that I am God: I will be exalted among the heathen, I will be exalted in the earth.

PSALM 46:10

JESUS, THE VERY THOUGHT OF THEE

Jesus, the very thought of Thee
With sweetness fills my breast;
But sweeter far Thy face to see
And in Thy presence rest.

No voice can sing, no heart can frame,
Or can the mem'ry find
A sweeter sound than Jesus' name,
O Saviour of mankind!

O Hope of ev'ry contrite heart,
O Joy of all the meek,
To those who fall how kind Thou art,
How good to those who seek.

But what to those who find, ah, this,
No tongue or pen can show.
The love of Jesus, what it is,
None but His loved ones know.

BERNARD OF CLAIRVAUX

PRAISING

You were praised, Lord.
When You entered Jerusalem
People shouted, "Hosanna,"
And strewed your path with palms;
And yet within days
Their shouts of praise rang hollow.

Lord, help me to praise God
For all His goodness
That has been shown to me.
I have sung His praises with delight.

Help me, in darker days,
When others mock or deride,
Not to be silent,
But continue to be loyal
In love and praise.

FRANK TOPPING

Whether therefore ye eat, or drink, or whatsoever ye do, do all to the glory of God.

1 CORINTHIANS 10:31

15

ON PRAISING GOD

IZAAK WALTON

Let not the blessings we receive daily from God make us not to value or not praise Him because they be common; let us not forget to praise Him for the innocent mirth and pleasure we have met with since we met together.

What would a blind man give to see the pleasant rivers and meadows and flowers and fountains that we have met since we met together!

I have been told, that if a man that was born blind could obtain to have his sight for only one hour during his whole life and should, at the first opening of his eyes, fix his sight upon the sun when it was in its full glory, either at rising or setting of it, he would be transported and amazed and so admire the glory of it that he would not willingly turn his eyes from that first ravishing object to behold all the other various beauties this world could present to him.

And this, and many other like blessings, we enjoy daily; and for most of them, because they are so common, most men forget to pay their praises, but let not us, because it is a sacrifice so pleasing to him that made the sun and us; and still protects us; and gives us flowers and showers, and stomachs and meat, and content, and leisure to go a-fishing.

I will praise thee, O LORD, with my whole heart; I will shew forth all thy marvellous works. I will be glad and rejoice in thee: I will sing praise to thy name, O thou most High.

PSALM 9:1–2

IT IS NOT FAR TO GO

It is not far to go,
    for you are near.
It is not far to go,
    for you are here.
And not by travelling, Lord,
    men come to you,
But by the way of love,
    and we love you.

AMY CARMICHAEL

PRAYER OF ADORATION

I adore Thee, Lord Jesus, dwelling in my heart.
I beseech Thee abide in me in all the tranquility of Thy power,
In all the perfection of Thy ways,
In all the brightness of Thy presence,
And in all the holiness of Thy Spirit:
That I may know the breadth and length
And depth and height of Thy love,
And do Thou trample down in me
All power of evil in the might of Thy Spirit
To the glory of God the Father.
Amen.

PÉRE OLIER

PRAISE, MY SOUL, THE KING OF HEAVEN

Praise, my soul, the King of heaven;
　To his feet thy tribute bring;
Ransomed, healed, restored, forgiven,
　Evermore His praises sing.
　　Alleluia! Alleluia!
　Praise the everlasting King.

Praise Him for His grace and favour
　To our fathers in distress;
Praise Him still the same as ever,
　Slow to chide and swift to bless.
　　Alleluia! Alleluia!
　Glorious in His faithfulness.

Father-like He tends and spares us;
　Well our feeble frame He knows;
In His hand He gently bears us,
　Rescues us from all our foes.
　　Alleluia! Alleluia!
　Widely yet His mercy flows.

Angels in the height adore Him!
　Ye behold Him face to face;
Saints triumphant bow before Him,
　Gathered in from every race.
　　Alleluia! Alleluia!
　Praise with us the God of grace.

HENRY F. LYTE

17

WE MAGNIFY THEE, O LORD

We magnify Thee, O Lord.
We bless the excellency of Thy name
In the great works of Thy hands:
The manifold vestures of earth
And sky and sea;
The course of the stars and light;
The songs of birds;
The hues of flowers;
The frame and attributes of everything
That has breath;
And, upholding all,
Thy wisdom, marvellous,
Worthy to be praised.

But most, that by Thy sure promise,
We now do only taste the glory
That shall be revealed
When Thou, O God,
Wilt take the power and reign,
World without end.
Amen.
AUTHOR UNKNOWN

A PRAYER OF PRAISE

Praised be Thou, O God, Almighty Ruler,
Who dost make the day
Bright with Thy sunshine
And the night with the beams
Of heavenly fires!

Listen now to our prayers,
And forgive us both our conscious
And unconscious transgressions.

Clothe us with the armour of righteousness;
Shield us with Thy truth;
Watch over us with Thy power;

Save us from all calamity;
And give us grace to pass
All the days of our life blameless,
Holy, peaceful, free from sin,
Terror, and offense.

For with Thee is mercy
And plenteous redemption,
Our Lord and God;

And to Thee we bring our thanks
And praise.
Amen.
AUTHOR UNKNOWN

THE HUNDRED SEVENTEENTH PSALM

Praise Him that aye
Remains the same:
All tongues display
Jehovah's fame.

Sing all that share
This earthly ball;

His mercies are
Exposed to all.

Like as the word
Once He doth give,
Rolled in record,
Doth time outlive.

MARY SIDNEY HERBERT

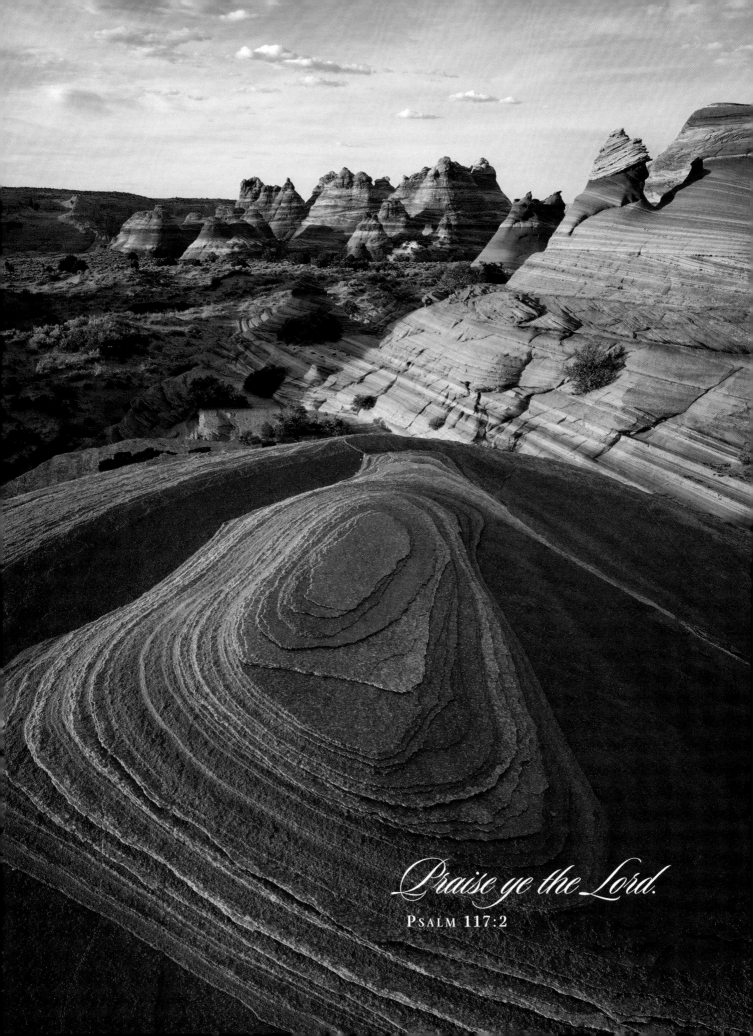

Praise ye the Lord.

PSALM 117:2

May all that He has created praise Him.

TERESA OF ÁVILA

LET US, WITH A GLADSOME MIND

Let us, with a gladsome mind,
Praise the Lord, for He is kind,
For His mercies still endure,
E'er faithful, ever sure.

Let us blaze His name abroad,
For of gods He is the God,
Who by all-commanding might,
Filled the new-made world with light.

He the golden tressed sun
Caused all day his course to run,

Th' horned moon to shine by night,
'Mid her spangled sisters bright.

He His chosen race did bless
In the wasteful wilderness;
He hath, with a piteous eye,
Looked upon our misery.

All things living He doth feed;
His full hand supplies their need,
For His mercies still endure,
Ever faithful, ever sure.

JOHN MILTON

A Prayer before Worship

O Lord our God,
Who has bidden the light
To shine out of darkness,
Who hast again awakened us
To praise Thy goodness
And ask for Thy grace:
Accept now, in Thy endless mercy,
The sacrifice of our worship
And thanksgiving;

And grant unto us all such requests
As may be wholesome for us.
Make us to be children of the light
And of the day, and heirs
Of Thy everlasting inheritance.

Remember, O Lord,
According to the multitude of Thy mercies,
Thy whole Church:
All who join with us in prayer;
All our brethren by land or sea,
Or wherever they may be
In Thy vast Kingdom, who stand in need
Of Thy grace and succour.

Pour out upon them the riches
Of Thy mercy, so that we,
Redeemed in soul and body,
And steadfast in faith,
May ever praise Thy wonderful
And holy name. Amen.

AUTHOR UNKNOWN

May You Be Blessed Forever, Lord

May You be blessed forever, Lord,
    for not abandoning me
    when I abandoned You.
May You be blessed forever, Lord,
    for offering Your hand of love
    in my darkest, most lonely moment.
May You be blessed forever, Lord,
    for putting up with
    such a stubborn soul as mine.
May You be blessed forever, Lord,
    for loving me
    more than I love myself.
May You be blessed forever, Lord,
    for continuing to pour out
    Your blessings upon me,
    even though I respond so poorly.
May You be blessed forever, Lord,
    for drawing out the goodness in all people,
    even including me.
May You be blessed forever, Lord,
    for repaying our sin
    with Your love.
May You be blessed forever, Lord,
    for being constant and unchanging,
    amidst all the changes of the world.
May You be blessed forever, Lord,
    for Your countless blessings on me
    and on all Your creatures.

TERESA OF ÁVILA

Thy Wonderful Works

Many, O LORD my God,
Are thy wonderful works
Which thou hast done,
And thy thoughts which are to us-ward:
They cannot be reckoned up
In order unto thee:
If I would declare and speak of them,
They are more than can be numbered.

PSALM 40:5

Prayer of Worship

AUTHOR UNKNOWN

O God of peace and charity! We beseech Thee holy Lord, Almighty Father, eternal God, that we may worship Thee with a pure heart. Let us dance before Thee with a clean conscience; let us serve Thee with all our strength.

We bless Thee, Holy Trinity; we give thanks to Thee; we praise Thee every day; we pray unto Thee "Abba, Father." May our praise be sweet to Thee and our prayer accepted.

God is a Sprit: and they that worship him must worship him in spirit and in truth.

JOHN 4:24

O Come, Let Us Sing

O come, let us sing unto the LORD:
Let us make a joyful noise
To the rock of our salvation.

Let us come before his presence
With thanksgiving,
And make a joyful noise
Unto him with psalms.

For the LORD is a great God,
And a great King above all gods.
In his hand are the deep places
Of the earth:

The strength of the hills is his also.
The sea is his, and he made it:
And his hands formed the dry land.

O come, let us worship
And bow down:
Let us kneel before the LORD our maker.

PSALM 95:1–6

A Third-Century Doxology

May none of God's wonderful works
    keep silence, night or morning.
Bright stars, high mountains,
    the depths of the seas,
    sources of rushing rivers:
May all these break into song
    as we sing to Father, Son,
    and Holy Spirit.
May all the angels in the heavens reply:
    Amen! Amen! Amen!
Power, praise, honour, eternal glory to God,
    the only Giver of grace.
    Amen! Amen! Amen!

AUTHOR UNKNOWN

Almighty One, in the woods I am blessed. Happy everyone in the woods. Every tree speaks of Thee. O God! What glory in the woodland! On the heights in peace—peace to serve Him.

LUDWIG VAN BEETHOVEN

Prayer for Acceptable Worship

William Bright

O Almighty God, from whom every good prayer cometh,
and who pourest out on all who desire it the spirit of grace and supplication,
deliver us, when we draw nigh to Thee, from coldness of heart and wanderings
of mind, that with steadfast thoughts and kindled affections we may worship
Thee in spirit and in truth; through Jesus Christ our Lord. Amen.

Thoughts in Solitude

Thomas Merton

Let this be my only consolation, that wherever I am You, my Lord, are
loved and praised. The trees indeed love You without knowing You. The tiger
lilies and cornflowers are there proclaiming that they love You, without being
aware of Your presence. The beautiful dark clouds ride slowly across the sky
musing on You like children who do not know what they are dreaming of as
they play.

But in the midst of them all, I know You, and I know of Your presence. In
them and in me I know of the love which they do not know, and, what is greater,
I am abashed by the presence of Your love in me. O kind and terrible love,
which You have given me and which could never be in my heart if You did not
love me! For in the midst of these beings which have never offended You, I am
loved by You, and it would seem most of all as one who has offended You. I am
seen by You under the sky, and my offenses have been forgotten by You—but I
have not forgotten them.

Only one thing I ask: that the memory of them should not make me afraid to
receive into my heart the gift of Love which You have replaced in me. I will
receive it because I am unworthy. In doing so I will only love You all the more
and give Your mercy greater glory.

Remembering that I have been a sinner, I will love You in spite of what I have
been, knowing that my love is precious because it is Yours, rather than my own.
Precious to You because it comes from Your own Son, but precious even more
because it makes me Your son.

A Prayer of Worship

Lord, be it Thine,
Unfaltering praise of mine!
To Thee my whole heart's love be given
Of earth and heaven Thou King divine.

Lord, be it Thine,
Unfaltering praise of mine!

And, O pure Prince, make clear my way
To serve and pray at Thy sole shrine.

Lord, be it Thine,
Unfaltering praise of mine!
O Father of souls that long,
Take this my song and make it Thine.
Author Unknown

OUR FATHER WHICH ART IN HEAVEN, HALLOWED BE THY NAME

ON TRUSTING GOD

JULIAN OF NORWICH

He said not: thou shalt not be tempted; thou shalt not be travailed; thou shalt not be afflicted. But He said: thou shalt not be overcome.

God willeth that we take heed of these words and that we be ever strong in such trust, in weal and woe. For He loveth and enjoyeth us, and so willeth He that we love and enjoy Him and mightily trust in Him, and all shall be well.

Trust in the LORD, *and do good;*
so shalt thou dwell in the land,
and verily thou shalt be fed.

PSALM 37:3

GOD IS MY STRONG SALVATION

God is my strong salvation;
What foe have I to fear?
In darkness and temptation
My light, my help is near.

Though hosts encamp around me,
Firm in the fight I stand;
What terror can confound me
With God at my right hand?

Place on the Lord reliance;
My soul with courage wait.
His truth be thine affiance
When faint and desolate;

His might thy heart shall strengthen;
His love thy joy increase;
Mercy thy days shall lengthen;
The Lord will give thee peace.

JAMES MONTGOMERY

KING OF GLORIE, KING OF PEACE

King of Glorie, King of Peace,
     I will love Thee;
And that love may never cease,
     I will move Thee.

Thou hast granted my request;
     Thou hast heard me.
Thou didst note my work breast;
     Thou hast spar'd me.

Wherefore with my utmost art
     I will sing Thee,
And the cream of all my heart
     I will bring Thee.

Small it is, in this poor sort
     To enroll Thee:
E'en eternitie's too short
     To extol Thee.

GEORGE HERBERT

In prayer it is better to have a heart
without words than words without a heart.

JOHN BUNYAN

The Earth Is the Lord's

The earth is the Lord's,
    and the fullness thereof;
    the world, and they that dwell therein.

For he hath founded it upon the seas,
    and established it upon the floods.

Who shall ascend into the hill of the Lord?
    or who shall stand in his holy place?

He that hath clean hands, and a pure heart;
    who hath not lifted up his soul
    unto vanity, nor sworn deceitfully.

He shall receive the blessing from the Lord,
    and righteousness
    from the God of his salvation.

This is the generation of them that seek him,
    that seek thy face, O Jacob.
    Selah.

Lift up your heads, O ye gates;
    and be ye lift up, ye everlasting doors;
    and the King of glory shall come in.

Who is this King of glory?
    The Lord strong and mighty,
    the Lord mighty in battle.

Lift up your heads, O ye gates;
    even lift them up, ye everlasting doors;
    and the King of glory shall come in.

Who is this King of glory?
    The Lord of hosts,
    he is the King of glory.
    Selah.

Psalm 24

God Is My Salvation

Behold, God is my salvation;
    I will trust, and not be afraid:
    for the Lord Jehovah is my strength
    and my song;
    he also is become my salvation.
Therefore with joy shall ye draw water
    out of the wells of salvation.
And in that day shall ye say,
    Praise the Lord,
    call upon his name,
    declare his doings among the people,
    make mention that his name is exalted.
Sing unto the Lord;
    for he hath done excellent things:
    this is known in all the earth.

Isaiah 12:2–5

I Am Trusting Thee, Lord Jesus

I am trusting Thee, Lord Jesus;
    At Thy feet I bow;
For Thy grace and tender mercy,
    Trusting now.

I am trusting Thee to guide me;
    Thou alone shalt lead,
Every day and hour supplying
    All my need.

I am trusting Thee, Lord Jesus;
    Never let me fall;
I am trusting Thee forever,
    And for all.

Frances R. Havergal

Trust in the Lord, and do good.

PSALM 37:3

A Prayer of Trust

ANNE BRADSTREET

Lord, why should I doubt anymore, when You have given me such assured pledges of Your love?

First, You are my Creator; I am Your creature: You my Master, I Your servant. But hence arises not my comfort: You are my Father; I am Your child.

"You shall be my sons and daughters," says the Lord Almighty. Christ is my brother: "I ascend to my Father and your Father, to my God and your God; but, lest this should not be enough, your maker is your husband."

Nay, more, I am a member of His body, He my head. Such privileges, had not the Word of truth made them known, who or where is the man that dared in his heart to have presumed to have thought it?

So wonderful are these thoughts that my spirit fails in me on their consideration, and I am confounded to think that God, who has done so much for me, should have so little from me.

But this is my comfort, that when I come to heaven, I shall understand perfectly what He has done for me, and then I shall be able to praise Him as I ought.

Lord, having this hope, let me purify myself as You are pure, and let me be no more afraid of death, but even desire to be dissolved and be with You which is best of all. Amen.

It is not our trust that keeps us, but the God in whom we trust who keeps us.
OSWALD CHAMBERS

For I Know the Thoughts

For I know the thoughts that I think toward you, saith the LORD,
Thoughts of peace, and not of evil, to give you an expected end.

Then shall ye call upon me, and ye shall go and pray unto me,
And I will hearken unto you.

And ye shall seek me, and find me,
When ye shall search for me with all your heart.
JEREMIAH 29:11–13

God Alone Suffices

Let nothing disturb you;
Let nothing dismay you;
All things pass.

God never changes.
Patience attains
All it strives for.
He who has God
Finds he lacks nothing;
God alone suffices.
TERESA OF ÁVILA

FAITH AND OBEDIENCE

CHAPTER TWO

*Thy kingdom come.
Thy will be done on earth,
as it is in heaven . . .*

*True faith is never found alone;
it is accompanied by expectation.*

MARTIN LUTHER

Somehow, while praying to God, it became clear to me that God is indeed a real Being. . . . And this is not a feeling, not an abstraction, but a real Being; and I have felt Him.
LEO TOLSTOY

TALKING WITH GOD

CHARLES STANLEY

Now it came to pass, as he was praying in a certain place, when he ceased, that one of his disciples said to him, "Lord, teach us to pray, as John also taught his disciples" (Luke 11:1–2).

Jesus' disciples had undoubtedly logged many hours in prayer by the time this exchange occurred. But after watching Jesus pray, they were keenly aware that something was different about the way He prayed. There was such a stark contrast that asking specific questions in an attempt to fine-tune their skills wasn't adequate. They needed a complete overhaul. So they said to Him, "Teach us to pray." In other words, "Let's start from the very beginning."

Jesus' response is somewhat surprising. The typical response to such a question today is, "It's easy. Prayer is just talking to God." Or you might hear someone say, "You don't learn to pray. You just pray. No one can teach another person to pray. It must come from the heart."

Jesus didn't trivialize their question. He took it seriously. His answer gives us the impression that He was waiting for them to ask. It was a lesson He had been looking forward to teaching for some time. And much to our surprise, He began by giving them the exact words to say, "When you pray, say . . ."

From there He went on to share several principles on prayer. He taught them to persevere (Luke 11:5–8). He explained and illustrated the sincere interest the heavenly Father took in the prayers of His children (Luke 11: 11–13). He promised them that their prayers would be heard and answered (Luke 11:9–10).

Prayer is something we learn to do. We are not born knowing how to pray. We are not even born again knowing how to pray. We, like the disciples, must learn to pray.

And it shall come to pass, that before they call, I will answer; and while they are yet speaking, I will hear.
ISAIAH 65:24

On Faith and Prayer

Norman Vincent Peale

Faith begins as a thin trickle across the mind. Repeated, it becomes habitual. It cuts into the consciousness until, as you deepen the channel, faith-thought overflows and whatever you think about yourself, about your family, about your business, about your future, about the world becomes optimistic and positive.

To be efficient in prayer you must learn the art of praying. You can read every book ever written about prayer, and you can attend innumerable discussions on prayer, but the only way to learn to pray is to pray.

Make your prayers simple and natural. Talk to God as to a friend.

I Will Lift Up Mine Eyes

I will lift up mine eyes unto the hills,
    from whence cometh my help.
My help cometh from the LORD,
    which made heaven and earth.
He will not suffer thy foot to be moved:
    he that keepeth thee will not slumber.

Behold, he that keepeth Israel
    shall neither slumber nor sleep.
The LORD is thy keeper: the LORD is thy shade
    upon thy right hand.
The sun shall not smite thee by day,
    nor the moon by night.

The LORD shall preserve thee from all evil:
    he shall preserve thy soul.
The LORD shall preserve thy going out
    and thy coming in from this time forth,
    and even for evermore.

PSALM 121

The Hundred Twenty-First Psalm

Up to those bright and gladsome hills
Whence flows my weal and mirth;
I look and sigh for Him, who fills
(Unseen) both heaven and earth.

The glorious God is my sole stay;
He is my sun and shade.
The cold by night, the heat by day,
Neither shall me invade.

He keeps me from the spite of foes,
Doth all their plots control,
And is a shield (not reckoning those)
Unto my very soul.

Whether abroad, amidst the crowd,
Or else within my door,
He is my pillar and my cloud,
Now and for evermore.

HENRY VAUGHAN

*The principle part
of faith is patience.*

GEORGE MACDONALD

Give Me a Full Faith

Give me, good Lord, a full faith,
    a firm hope and a fervent charity,
    a love to Thee incomparable
    above the love to myself. Amen.
Thomas More

We Walk by Faith

We walk by faith and not by sight;
No gracious words we hear
From Him who spoke as none e'er spoke,
But we believe Him near.

We may not touch His hands and side,
Nor follow where He trod;
But in His promise we rejoice
And cry, "My Lord and God!"

Help then, O Lord, our unbelief;
And may our faith abound
To call on You when You are near
And seek where You are found;

That when our life of faith is done,
In realms of clearer light
We may behold You as You are,
With full and endless sight.
Henry Alford

Prayer for a Childlike Faith

Father, let me hold Thy hand
    and like a child walk with Thee
    down all my days,
    secure in Thy love and strength.
Thomas À Kempis

Prayer for Strengthened Faith

God, the Father of our Lord Jesus Christ,
    increase in us faith and truth and gentleness
    and grant us part and lot among the saints. Amen.
Polycarp

Faith Is

Now faith is the substance of things hoped for,
    the evidence of things not seen.
For by it the elders obtained a good report.
Through faith we understand that the worlds
    were framed by the word of God,
    so that things which are seen
    were not made of things which do appear.
Hebrews 11:1–3

That Christ May Dwell in Your Hearts by Faith

That Christ may dwell in your hearts by faith;
    that ye, being rooted and grounded in love,
May be able to comprehend with all saints
    what is the breadth, and length,
    and depth, and height;
And to know the love of Christ,
    which passeth knowledge,
    that ye might be filled with all the fullness of God.
Ephesians 3:17–19

37

Thy kingdom come. Thy will be done on earth, as it is in heaven   Faith

The Difficulties of Praying

Henri J. Nouwen

Why, O Lord, is it so hard for me to keep my heart directed toward You? Why do the many little things I want to do, and the many people I know, keep crowding into my mind, even during the hours that I am totally free to be with You and You alone? Why does my mind wander off in so many directions, and why does my heart desire the things that lead me astray? Are You not enough for me? Do I keep doubting Your love and care, Your mercy and grace? Do I keep wondering, in the center of my being, whether You will give me all I need if I just keep my eyes on You?

Please accept my distractions, my fatigue, my irritations, and my faithless wanderings. You know me more deeply and fully than I know myself. You love me with a greater love than I can love myself. You even offer me more than I can desire.

Look at me, see me in all my misery and inner confusion, and let me sense Your presence in the midst of my turmoil. All I can do is show myself to You. Yet, I am afraid to do so. I am afraid that You will reject me. But I know—with the knowledge of faith—that You desire to give me Your love. The only thing You ask of me is not to hide from You, not to run away in despair, not to act as if You were a relentless despot.

Take my tired body, my confused mind, and my restless soul into Your arms and give me rest, simple quiet rest. Do I ask too much too soon? I should not worry about that. You will let me know. Come, Lord Jesus, come. Amen.

That the trial of your faith, being much more precious than of gold that perisheth, though it be tried with fire, might be found unto the praise and honor and glory at the appearing of Jesus Christ.

1 Peter 1:7

Escape to Prayer

Come now, little man, turn aside
    for a while from your daily employment,
    escape for a moment
    from the tumult of your thoughts.
Put aside your weighty cares,
    let your burdensome distractions wait,
    free yourself awhile for God,
    and rest awhile in Him.

Enter the inner chamber of your soul,
    shut out everything except God
    and that which can help you in seeking Him,
    and when you have shut the door, seek Him.
Now, my whole heart, say to God,
    "I seek your face,
    Lord, it is your face I seek."

Anselm

Teach me to breathe deeply in faith.

SØREN KIERKEGAARD

THE EIGHTY-FIRST PSALM

In God our strength, let us rejoice;
To Jacob's God, let us now sing;
And in our psalms, to help the voice,
The timbrel, harp, and psaltery bring.
The moon renewing, trumpets blow,
And when the solemn feastings be:
For Jacob's God, long time ago,
    In Israel did this law decree.

This testimony He prepared,
When Joseph came from Egypt land
And lived where he a language heard,
Whose words he did not understand.
From burdens and the potters task,
Thy hands and shoulders I did free;
I helped when thou for help didst ask,
    And heard thee from the storm, said He.
    Selah.

Even at the waters of debate
I said (that I might prove thee there)

O Israel, mark what I relate,
And to my words incline thine ear.
Thou shalt no other gods at all,
But me the Lord thy God receive;
For thee I brought from Egypt's thrall,
    And will thy largest askings give.

But Israel did my words contemn;
Of me, my people would have none:
So, to their pleasures left I them,
Who after their own lusts are gone.
Oh! had my people me obeyed,
If Israel had my ways pursued,
I on their foes my hand had laid:
    Their haters I had soon subdued.

My foes had then obeyed my power,
And I had still my folk upheld:
I then had fed with purest flour
    And, with rock-honey, them had filled.
GEORGE WITHER

Sing Aloud unto God

Sing aloud unto God our strength:
  make a joyful noise unto the God of Jacob.
Take a psalm, and bring hither the timbrel,
  the pleasant harp with the psaltery.
Blow up the trumpet in the new moon,
  in the time appointed, on our solemn feast day.
For this was a statute for Israel, and a law
  of the God of Jacob.
This he ordained in Joseph for a testimony,
  when he went out through the land of Egypt:
  where I heard a language that I understood not.
I removed his shoulder from the burden:
  his hands were delivered from the pots.
Thou callest in trouble, and I delivered thee;
  I answered thee in the secret place of thunder:
  I proved thee at the waters of Meribah.
    Selah.
Hear, O my people, and I will testify unto thee:
  O Israel, if thou wilt hearken unto me;
There shall no strange god be in thee;
  neither shalt thou worship any strange god.
I am the LORD thy God, which brought thee out
  of the land of Egypt: open thy mouth wide,
  and I will fill it.
But my people would not hearken to my voice;
  and Israel would none of me.
So I gave them up unto their own hearts' lust:
  and they walked in their own counsels.
Oh that my people had hearkened unto me,
  and Israel had walked in my ways!
I should soon have subdued their enemies,
  and turned my hand against their adversaries.
The haters of the LORD should have submitted
  themselves unto him:
  but their time should have endured for ever.
He should have fed them also with the finest of the wheat:
  and with honey out of the rock should I have satisfied thee.
PSALM 81

Thy Will Be Done

Thy will be done as 'tis in heaven,
By every creature here below;
Thy will be done, my loving Father,
From whom all grace and blessings flow.

Even to highest heaven,
Loud let our voices ring:
Thy will be done, Thou art our Father;
Thy will be done, Thou art our King.
Thy will be done, Thou art our Father;
Thy will be done, Thou art our King.

When from our hearts all joy seems fading,
When griefs and trials, one by one,
O'erwhelm our souls; then in our sorrow,
Teach us to say, "Thy will be done."

Even to highest heaven,
Loud let our voices ring:
Thy will be done, Thou art our Father;
Thy will be done, Thou art our King.
Thy will be done, Thou art our Father;
Thy will be done, Thou art our King.

In joy or grief, whate'er befall us,
E'en till the sands of life be run,
In life and death this is our watchword:
"Thy will be done; thy will be done."

Even to highest heaven,
Loud let our voices ring:
Thy will be done, Thou art our Father;
Thy will be done, Thou art our King.
Thy will be done, Thou art our Father;
Thy will be done, Thou art our King.
ISAAC WILLIAMS

A Prayer of Submission

Queen Anne

 and eternal God, the disposer of all the affairs of the world, there is not one circumstance so great as not to be subject to Thy power, nor so small but it comes within Thy care; Thy goodness and wisdom show themselves through all Thy words, and Thy lovingkindness and mercy appear in the several dispensations of Thy providence. May we readily submit ourselves to Thy pleasure and sincerely resign our wills to Thine, with all patience, meekness, and humility.

Keep My Commandments

If ye love me, keep my commandments.
And I will pray the Father,
    and he shall give you another Comforter,
    that he may abide with you for ever;
Even the Spirit of truth;
    whom the world cannot receive,
    because it seeth him not, neither knoweth him:
    but ye know him; for he dwelleth with you,
    and shall be in you.
I will not leave you comfortless: I will come to you.
John 14:15–18

Speak, Lord

Speak, Lord, for Thy servant heareth.
Grant us ears to hear,
    eyes to see,
    wills to obey,
    hearts to love;
Then declare what Thou wilt,
    reveal what Thou wilt,
    command what Thou wilt,
    demand what Thou wilt.
    Amen.
Christina Rossetti

Teach Us, Lord

Teach us, Lord,
To serve You as You deserve,
To give and not to count the cost,
To fight and not to heed the wounds,
To toil and not to seek for rest,
To labor and not to ask for any reward
Save that of knowing that we do Your will.
Amen.
Ignatius of Loyola

43

Thy kingdom come. Thy will be done on earth, as it is in heaven   Obedience

BLESS THE LORD

PSALM 103

Bless the Lord, O my soul: and all that is within me,
    bless his holy name.

Bless the LORD, O my soul, and forget not all his benefits:

Who forgiveth all thine iniquities; who healeth all thy diseases;

Who redeemeth thy life from destruction; who crowneth thee with loving
    kindness and tender mercies;

Who satisfieth thy mouth with good things; so that thy youth is renewed
    like the eagle's.

The LORD executeth righteousness and judgment for all that are oppressed.

He made known his ways unto Moses, his acts unto the children of Israel.

The LORD is merciful and gracious, slow to anger, and plenteous in mercy.

He will not always chide: neither will he keep his anger for ever.

He hath not dealt with us after our sins; nor rewarded us according to
    our iniquities.

For as the heaven is high above the earth, so great is his mercy toward them
    that fear him.

As far as the east is from the west, so far hath he removed our transgressions
    from us.

Like as a father pitieth his children, so the LORD pitieth them that fear him.

For he knoweth our frame; he remembereth that we are dust.

As for man, his days are as grass: as a flower of the field, so he flourisheth.

For the wind passeth over it, and it is gone; and the place thereof shall know
    it no more.

But the mercy of the LORD is from everlasting to everlasting upon them that
    fear him, and his righteousness unto children's children;

To such as keep his covenant, and to those that remember his commandments
    to do them.

The LORD hath prepared his throne in the heavens; and his kingdom ruleth
    over all.

Bless the LORD, ye his angels, that excel in strength, that do his commandments,
    hearkening unto the voice of his word.

Bless ye the LORD, all ye his hosts; ye ministers of his, that do his pleasure.

Bless the LORD, all his works in all places of his dominion: bless the LORD,
    O my soul.

THE HUNDRED THIRD PSALM

My soul, with all thy powers thy maker praise;
Forget not all His benefits to thee,
Who pardons all thy sins and doth thee raise
When thou art fallen through any infirmity,
Who doth thee save from mischiefs that would kill thee
And crowneth thee with mercies ever more,
And with the best of things doth feed and fill thee
And eagle-like thy youth and strength restore.

When men oppressed do to Him appeal,
He righteth every one against his foe:
He unto Moses did His laws reveal,
And unto Jacob's race His works did show.
He is more full of grace than we of sin,
To anger slow, compassionate and kind;
He doth not ever chide and never lin,
Nor keeps displeasure always in His mind
Nor after our misdeeds doth He us charge,
Nor takes He of our faults a strict account.
But as the space from earth to heaven is large,
So far His mercy doth our sins surmount.

As east from west is distant far away,
So far doth He from us our sins remove;

As fathers' kindness to their sons bewray,
So God, to them that fear Him, shows His love.
For He that made us, and knows all, doth know
The matter whereof man was made of old:
That we were formed here on earth below
Of dust and clay, and of no better mold.

Man's age doth wither as the fading grass;
He flourisheth but as the flower in May,
Which when the south wind over it doth pass
Is gone, and where it grew no man can say.
But God's sweet kindness ever doth consist;
His truth from age to age continue shall
To them that in His righteous laws persist,
And think upon them to perform them all.

Heaven is God's seat; there doth His glory dwell,
But over all His empire doth extend.
Praise Him ye angels which in strength excel,
And His command do evermore attend.
Praise Him ye hosts of heaven which serve Him there,
Whose service with His pleasure doth accord;
And praise Him all His creatures everywhere,
And thou, my soul, for thy part praise the Lord.
JOHN DAVIES

Obedience is the eye of the spirit.

SAMUEL DICKEY GORDON

PRAYER TO BE USED IN GOD'S SERVICE

Use me then, my Saviour, for whatever purpose
    and in whatever way Thou mayest require.
Here is my poor heart, an empty vessel;
    fill it with Thy grace.
Here is my sinful and troubled soul;
    quicken it and refresh it with Thy love.
Take my heart for Thine abode,
    my mouth to spread abroad the glory of Thy name,
    my love and all my powers
    for the advancement of Thy believing people,
    and never suffer the steadfastness and
    confidence of my faith to abate—
    so that at all times I may be enabled
    from the heart to say, Jesus needs me,
    and I Him. Amen.

DWIGHT LYMAN MOODY

LORD, MAKE ME AN INSTRUMENT OF YOUR PEACE

Lord, make me an instrument of Your peace.
Where there is hatred, let me sow love,
Where there is injury, pardon,
Where there is doubt, faith,
Where there is despair, hope,
Where there is darkness, light,
Where there is sadness, joy.

O Divine Master, grant that I may
Not so much seek to be consoled as to console,
Not so much to be understood as to understand,
Not so much to be loved as to love;

For it is in giving that we receive,
It is in pardoning that we are pardoned,
It is in dying that we awake to eternal life.

FRANCIS OF ASSISI

Prayer

Author Unknown

Almighty God, by Thy Spirit teach me what is wise and what is foolish, what is noble and what is mean, what is eternal and what is passing.

And if Thou findest that Thy greatest things are not my greatest, and that the sweetest things of Thy world are not sweetest to me, have mercy. Make me wise to know what I would soonest part with: whether, if the choice were given me, I would rather part with truth than wealth; whether I desire more the honors of the world than the hidden manna and the name written in the book of life.

May I prefer goodness to greatness, pureness to pride, worthiness to wealth, the doing of one good thing to the hearing of many great ones: rather to be of Thy unknown known ones written in Thy book of life than to have my name written in the book of earthly fame. Amen.

If ye be willing and obedient, ye shall eat the good of the land.

ISAIAH 1:19

Prayer for Guidance

O Lord, You know what is best for me.
Let this or that be done as You please.
Give what You will, how much You will,
    and when You will.

THOMAS à KEMPIS

Prayer of Surrender

Take, Lord, all my liberty,
    my memory,
    my understanding,
    and my whole will.
You have given me all that I have,
    all that I am,
    and I surrender all to Your divine will,
    that You dispose of me.
Give me only Your love and Your grace.
With this I am rich enough,
    and I have no more to ask.
Amen.

IGNATIUS OF LOYOLA

Happy Is the Man

Happy is the man that findeth wisdom,
    and the man that getteth understanding.
For the merchandise of it is better
    than the merchandise of silver,
    and the gain thereof than fine gold.
She is more precious than rubies:
    and all the things thou canst desire
    are not to be compared unto her.
Length of days is in her right hand;
    and in her left hand riches and honour.
Her ways are ways of pleasantness,
    and all her paths are peace.
She is a tree of life to them that lay hold upon her:
    and happy is every one that retaineth her.
The LORD by wisdom hath founded the earth;
    by understanding hath he established the heavens.

PROVERBS 3:13–19

PRAYER TO THE UNCHANGING GOD

TERESE OF LISIEUEX

I have realized that whoever undertakes to do anything for the sake of earthly things or to earn the praise of others deceives himself. Today one thing pleases the world, tomorrow another; and what is praised on one occasion is denounced on another.

Blessed are You my Lord and my God, for You are unchangeable for all eternity. Whoever serves You faithfully to the end will enjoy life without end in eternity. Amen.

I can do all things through Christ which strengtheneth me.

PHILIPPIANS 4:13

THE CROSS, THE INSPIRATION

SAMUEL McCOMB

O God, our Refuge and our Strength! Thou art so high that the very Heaven of heavens cannot contain Thee, yet dost Thou dwell with him that is of a contrite and humble spirit. Thou livest in eternity; we are the creatures of a moment. Yet Thou has committed to us the solemn tasks of love and duty.

Though we fail and forget, Thou remainest faithful. Thou dost not despair when Thou findest us degraded and miserable in our sin, but bringest us forgiveness and hope. We are overwhelmed, O Lord, with wonder, to think that Thou dost believe in us and wilt not let us go. From the pleasures of sin, from the torment of guilt, from poverty and blighted hopes and ill-requited love, we turn to Thee, our Father, for comfort and satisfaction.

Make clear to us how the evils of the soul war against our happiness and health, how we are so fearfully and wonderfully made that not a wrong thought or base desire or strained emotion but leaves its mark upon our bodies. Take possession of us, and so inspire us with great thoughts and noble aspirations and unselfish feelings that our bodies may become fit temples for the habitation of Thy good Spirit. So occupy us with self-forgetting service for Thee that no time or strength may remain for our besetting sins.

Lay upon us the burdens of the weak, the crosses of other lives. Are any sick? Let us bring to them help and good cheer, and, if it may be, some gift of healing. Are there any naked and hungry? Let us clothe and feed them. Are there any

sad and depressed? Give to us the insight and sympathy in the presence of which the burdened heart will be eased and the darkened mind illumined.

Are there any remorseful and despairing? Speak to them through us, as Thy messengers, and say, I am thy salvation. Thus may the fires of a Christlike charity burn with a steady flame within us, and thus may our souls be kept pure and fresh and strong. O true and holy Light that lightenest every man, shine into these hearts of ours that we may hold converse with the sinful yet contract no stain, that we may share the pleasures and mingle in the noise and dust of life yet keep our garments unspotted from the world.

Forgive us that we have sinned so often against those around us by failing to draw near to them and to understand them, by want of pity for their trials and sorrows, by passing on our heedless way with no ear for the still, sad voices of weary and laden souls.

Henceforth let us be at one with the mind that was in Christ Jesus, who came not to be ministered unto, but to minister, and to give His life a ransom for many. Let the glory of His cross be the inspiration of all our thought and service, that suffering with Him here, we may reign with Him hereafter.

Hear us and answer us, for His sake. Amen.

Take My Life and Let It Be

Frances R. Havergal

Take my life, and let it be consecrated, Lord, to Thee. Take my moments and my days; let them flow in ceaseless praise. Take my hands, and let them move at the impulse of Thy love. Take my feet, and let them be swift and beautiful for Thee.

Take my voice, and let me sing, always, only, for my King. Take my lips, and let them be filled with messages from Thee. Take my silver and my gold, not a mite would I withhold. Take my intellect, and use every power as Thou shalt choose.

Take my will, and make it Thine; it shall be no longer mine. Take my heart; it is Thine own; it shall be Thy royal throne. Take my love, my Lord; I pour at Thy feet its treasure-store. Take myself, and I will be ever, only, all for Thee.

On the Christian Home

Holy is the true light, and passing wonderful,
Lending radiance to them that endured
   in the heat of the conflict.
From Christ they inherit a home of unfailing splendour
Wherein they rejoice with gladness evermore.
Salisbury Diurnal

Prayer for Strength and Dedication

Each day I pray: God give me strength anew
To do the task I do not wish to do,
To measure what I am by what I give—
God give me strength that I may rightly live.
Author Unknown

A Prayer for Submission

Blaise Pascal

O Lord, let me not henceforth desire health or life except to spend them for You, with You, and in You. You alone know what is good for me; do therefore what seems best to You.

Give to me or take from me; conform my will to Yours; and grant that with humble and perfect submission and in holy confidence I may receive the orders of Your eternal providence and may equally adore all that comes to me from You. Amen.

Obedience is the key to every door.

GEORGE MacDONALD

A PRAYER

I bind unto myself today the power of God
   To hold and lead:
   His eye to watch, His might to stay,
   His ear to hearken to my need,
   The wisdom of my God to teach,
   His hand to guide, His shield to ward,
   The word of God to give me speech,
   His heav'nly host to be my guard.
   Christ be with me,
   Christ within me,
   Christ behind me,
   Christ before me,
   Christ beside me, Christ to win me,
   Christ to comfort me and restore me,
   Christ beneath me, Christ above me,
   Christ in the hearts of all that love me,
   Christ in the mouth of friend and stranger.
PATRICK OF IRELAND

PRAYER FOR SELFLESSNESS

Sever me from myself
That I may be grateful to You;
May I perish to myself
That I may be safe in You;
May I die to myself
That I may live in You;
May I wither to myself
That I may blossom in You;
May I be emptied of myself
That I may abound in You;
May I be nothing to myself
That I may be all to You.
Amen.
DESIDERIUS ERASMUS

Prayer of Dedication

Henry Ward Beecher

Thou hast called us to Thyself, most merciful Father, with love and with promises abundant; and we are witnesses that it is not in vain that we draw near to Thee. We bear witness to Thy faithfulness. Thy promises are "Yea" and "Amen." Thy blessings are exceeding abundant more than we know or think.

We thank Thee for the privilege of prayer and for Thine answers to prayer, and we rejoice that Thou dost not answer according to our petitions. We are blind and are constantly seeking things which are not best for us. If Thou didst grant all our desires according to our requests, we should be ruined.

In dealing with our little children we give them, not the things which they ask for, but the things which we judge best for them; and Thou, our Father, art by Thy providence overruling our ignorance and our headlong mistakes and are doing for us, not so much the things that we request of Thee, as the things that we should ask. And we are, day by day, saved from peril and from ruin by Thy better knowledge and by Thy careful love. Amen.

Prayer for the Seasons of Life

Thomas Aquinas

Loving God, who sees in us nothing that You have not given Yourself, make my body healthy and agile, my mind sharp and clear, my heart joyful and contented, my soul faithful and loving. And surround me with the company of men and angels who share my devotion to You.

Above all, let me live in Your presence, for with You all fear is banished, and there is only harmony and peace. Let every day combine the beauty of spring, the brightness of summer, the abundance of autumn, and the repose of winter. And at the end of my life on earth, grant that I may come to see and to know You in the fullness of Your glory. Amen.

Teach Us to Pray

Peter Marshall

Lord, teach us to pray. Some of us are not skilled in the art of prayer. As we draw near to Thee in thought, our spirits long for Thy Spirit and reach out for Thee, longing to feel Thee near. We know not how to express the deepest emotions that lie hidden in our hearts.

In these moments, we have no polished phrases with which to impress one another, no finely molded, delicately turned clauses to present to Thee. Nor would we be confined to conventional petitions and repeat our prayers like the unwinding of a much-exposed film. We know, our Father, that we are praying most when we are saying least. We know that we are closest to Thee when we have left behind the things that have held us captive so long.

We would not be ignorant in prayer and, like children, make want lists for Thee. Rather, we pray that Thou wilt give unto us only what we really need. We would not make our prayers the importuning of Thee, an omnipotent God, to do what we want Thee to do. Rather, give us the vision, the courage, that shall enlarge our horizons and stretch our faith to the adventure of seeking Thy loving will for our lives.

We thank Thee that Thou art hearing us even now. We thank Thee for the grace of prayer. We thank Thee for Thyself.

REQUEST AND THANKSGIVING

CHAPTER THREE

Give us this day our daily bread . . .

To be efficient in prayer you must learn the art of praying. . . .
the only way to learn to pray is to pray. Make your prayers
simple and natural. Talk to God as to a friend.

POWER OF PRAYER

BILLY GRAHAM

In our modern age we have learned to harness the power of
the mighty Niagara and turn its force to beneficial use. We have learned to hold
steam captive in boilers and release its tremendous energy to turn our
machines and pull our trains. We have learned to contain gasoline vapors in a
cylinder and explode them at the appointed second to move our automobiles
and trucks along our highways. We have even discovered the secret of releasing
energy in the atom, which is capable of lighting cities, operating great indus-
tries, or destroying entire cities and civilizations.

But very few of us have learned how to fully develop the power of prayer.

Effectual prayer is offered in faith. Jesus said, "I tell you, whatever you ask for
in prayer, believe that you have received it, and it will be yours" (Mark 11:24).
James wrote: "If any of you lacks wisdom, he should ask God, who gives gener-
ously to all without finding fault, and it will be given to him. But when he asks,
he must believe and not doubt, because he who doubts is like a wave of the sea,
blown and tossed by the wind" (James 1:5, 6). If our prayers are aimless, mean-
ingless, and mingled with doubt, they will be unanswered. Prayer is more than
a wish turned heavenward: it is the voice of faith directed Godward.

What a privilege is yours—the privilege of prayer! In the light of coming
events, examine your heart, re-consecrate your life, yield yourself to God unre-
servedly, for only those who pray through a clean heart will be heard of Him. The
Bible says, "The prayer of a righteous man is powerful and effective" (James 5:16).

We are to pray not only for our own needs but for the needs of others. We
are to pray in times of adversity, lest we become faithless and unbelieving. We
are to pray in times of prosperity, lest we become boastful and proud. We are to
pray in times of danger, lest we become fearful and doubting. We need to pray
in times of security, lest we become careless and self-sufficient.

"More things are wrought by prayer than this world dreams of." Tennyson's
well-known words are no mere cliche. They state a sober truth. Bible teaching,
church history, Christian experience, all confirm that prayer does work. But as

56

REQUEST   TREASURY OF PRAYER we relate this matter of prayer specifically to the subject of suffering, we need to keep in mind several things which we have already stated and which we now summarize.

For one thing, we must always remember that prayer does not work automatically, nor is it a piece of spiritual magic. It's not like pressing an electric button and expecting an immediate response. We can't manipulate God or dictate to Him. He is sovereign, and we must recognize His sovereign rights.

This means, as we have stressed all along, that our prayers are subject to His will. And we should be glad of that. It takes the burden off ourselves and places it on the Lord. To say "Thy will be done" is not a sigh, but a song because His will is always what is best—both for us and those for whom we pray. As Dante said, "in His will is our peace." As believers we cannot find true peace outside the will of God.

Again, we may be sure that God is true to His Word and answers all sincere prayer offered in the name of the Lord Jesus Christ. But His answer is not always the same. As is so often pointed out, His answer may not necessarily be "Yes." It may be "No" or it may be "Wait." If it is "No" or "Wait," we have no right to say that God has not answered our prayer. It simply means that the answer is different from what we expected. We must get rid of the idea that if only we pray hard and long enough, God will always give us what we ask for in the end.

As we have seen, when we pray for help in trouble or for healing in sickness or for deliverance in persecution, God may not give us what we ask for, for that may not be His wise and loving will for us. But He will answer our prayer in His own way. He will not let us down in our hour of need. He will give us the patience, courage, and strength to endure our suffering; the ability to rise above it; and the assurance of His presence in all that we are called to pass through.

In any case, let us never forget that prayer is not just asking God for things. It's far bigger and better than that. At its deepest level, prayer is fellowship with God: enjoying His company, waiting upon His will, thanking Him for His mercies, committing our lives to Him, talking to Him about other people as well as ourselves, and listening in the silence for what He has to say to us.

This is what makes prayer so real and precious a thing, especially in times of stress and strain. When we come to the end of ourselves, we come to the beginning of God. As it has been said, our little things are all big to God's love; our big things are all small to His power.

You are denying yourself a marvelous privilege if you don't pray. The path of prayer is always open, whatever your need. Take it to the Lord in prayer!

THE TWENTY-EIGHTH PSALM

Hear, Lord my strength, the cries I make to Thee;
I am but dead if Thou seem deaf to me.
Hear when with humble prayer I Thee entreat,
With lifted hand before Thy mercy seat;

But rank me not with those which wicked are,
Whose lips speak peace, whose hearts are full of war;
According to their actions let them speed,
And as their merit is, so make their meed.

For that they see Thy works, and yet neglect them,
Thou shalt destroy and never more erect them;
The Lord be praised who hath vouchsafed to hear
And lend unto my prayer a gracious ear.

His shield protects, His strength doth me advance;
My tongue shall sing His praise, my heart shall dance:
He to His servants force and virtue gives,
Through Him in safety His anointed lives.

Save Thy peculiar people Lord, and bless them,
And lift their heads above them that oppress them.
JOHN DAVIES

OUT OF THE DEPTHS HAVE I CRIED

Out of the depths have I cried
    unto thee, O LORD.
Lord hear my voice: let thine ears
    be attentive to the voice
    of my supplications.
If thou, LORD, shouldest mark iniquities,
    O LORD, who shall stand?
But there is forgiveness with thee,
    that thou mayest be feared.
I wait for the LORD, my soul doth wait,
    and in his word do I hope.
My soul waiteth for the LORD
    more than they that watch
    for the morning:
    I say, more than they that watch
    for the morning.
Let Israel hope in the LORD:
    for with the LORD there is mercy,
    and with him is plenteous redemption.
And he shall redeem Israel
    from all his iniquities.
PSALM 130

UNTO THEE WILL I CRY

Unto thee will I cry, O LORD my rock;
   be not silent to me:
   lest, if thou be silent to me,
   I become like them
   that go down into the pit.
Hear the voice of my supplications,
   when I cry unto thee,
   when I lift up my hands
   toward thy holy oracle.
Draw me not away with the wicked,
   and with the workers of iniquity,
   which speak peace to their neighbours,
   but mischief is in their hearts.
Give them according to their deeds,
   and according to the wickedness
   of their endeavours:
   give them after the work of their hands;
   render to them their desert.
Because they regard not the works of the LORD,
   nor the operation of his hands,
   he shall destroy them,
   and not build them up.
Blessed be the LORD, because he hath heard
   the voice of my supplications.
The LORD is my strength and my shield;
   my heart trusted in him, and I am helped:
   therefore my heart greatly rejoiceth;
   and with my song will I praise him.
The LORD is their strength, and he is
   the saving strength of his anointed.
Save thy people, and bless thine inheritance:
   feed them also, and lift them up for ever.

PSALM 28

Lord, either lighten my burden
or strengthen my back.

THOMAS FULLER

Behold my needs which I know not myself.

FRANCOIS FENELON

THE HUNDRED THIRTIETH PSALM

From depth of sin and from a deep despair,
   From depth of death, from depth of heart's sorrow,
   From this deep cave of darkness deep repair,
Thee have I called, O Lord, to be my borrow;
   Thou in my voice, O Lord, perceive and hear
   My heart, my hope, my plaint, my overthrow,
My will to rise, and let by grant appear
   That to my voice Thine ears do well intend.
   No place so far that to Thee is not near,
No depth so deep that Thou mayst not extend
   Thine ear thereto: hear then my woeful plaint.
   For, Lord, if Thou do observe what men offend
And put Thy native mercy in restraint,
   If just exaction demand recompense,
   Who may endure, O Lord? Who shall not faint
At such account? Dread, and not reverence,
   Should so reign large. But Thou seeks rather love,
   For in Thy hand is mercy's residence,
By hope whereof Thou dost our hearts move.
   I in Thee, Lord, have set my confidence,
   My soul such trust doth evermore approve.
Thy holy word of eternal excellence,
   Thy mercy's promise, that is always just,
   Have been my stay, my pillar, and pretense.
My soul in God hath more desirous trust
   Than hath the watchman looking for the day
   By the relief to quench of sleep the thrust.
Let Israel trust unto the Lord alway,
   For grace and favor are His property:
   Plenteous ransom shall come with Him I say,
And shall redeem all our iniquity.

THOMAS WYATT

GIVE US THIS DAY OUR DAILY BREAD

Out of the Depths

Out of the depths I cry to Thee,
    Lord God! Oh hear my prayer!
Incline a gracious ear to me,
    And bid me not despair.
If Thou rememberest each misdeed,
If each should have its rightful meed,
    Lord, who shall stand before Thee!

'Tis through Thy love alone we gain
    The pardon of our sin;
The strictest life is but in vain;
    Our works can nothing win,
That none should boast himself of aught,
But own in fear Thy grace hath wrought
    What in him seemeth righteous.

Wherefore my hope is in the Lord,
    My works I count but dust.
I build not there, but on His word,
    And in His goodness trust.
Up to His care myself I yield;
He is my tower, my rock, my shield,
    And for His help I tarry.

Though great our sins and sore our wounds
    And deep dark our fall,
His helping mercy hath no bounds;
    His love surpasseth all.
Our truly loving Shepherd He,
Who shall at last set Israel free
    From all their sin and sorrow.
MARTIN LUTHER

O Lord, help me not to despise or oppose
what I do not understand.
WILLIAM PENN

Cast Thy Burden on the Lord

Cast thy burden on the Lord;
Only lean upon His word:
Thou shalt soon have cause to bless
His eternal faithfulness.

Ever in the raging storm
Thou shalt see His cheering form,
Hear His pledge of coming aid:
"It is I, be not afraid."

Cast thy burden at His feet;
Linger at His mercy seat:
He will lead thee by the hand
Gently to the better land.

He will gird thee by His power,
In thy weary, fainting hour:
Lean, then, loving, on His word;
Cast thy burden on the Lord.
AUTHOR UNKNOWN

Prayer for the Day's Mercy

Who can tell what a day may bring forth?
Cause me therefore, gracious God,
To live every day as if it were to be my last,
For I know not but that it may be such.

Cause me to live now as I shall wish
I had done when I come to die.
Oh grant that I may not die with any guilt
On my conscience or any known sin
Unrepented of, but that I may be found
In Christ, who is my only Saviour
And Redeemer.
THOMAS À KEMPIS

FOR CONSOLATION

AUTHOR UNKNOWN

O God, help me to think of Thee in this bitter trial. Thou knowest how my heart is rent with grief. In my weakness, tested so severely in soul by this visitation, I cry unto Thee, Father of all life: give me fortitude to say with Thy servant Job: "The Lord hath given; the Lord hath taken away; blessed be the name of the Lord."

Forgive the thoughts of my rebellious soul. Pardon me in these first hours of my grief, if I question Thy wisdom and exercise myself in things too high for me. Grant me strength to rise above this trial, to bear with humility life's sorrows and disappointments. Be nigh unto me, O God. Bring consolation and peace to my soul.

Praised art Thou, O God, who comfortest the mourners. Amen.

61

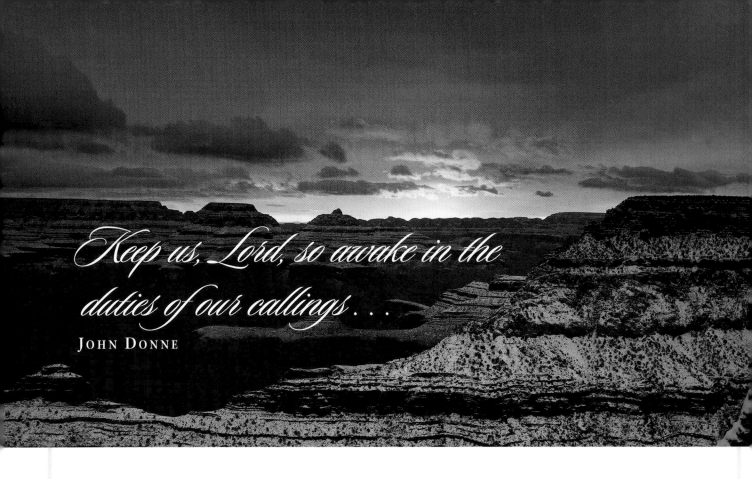

Keep us, Lord, so awake in the duties of our callings...

JOHN DONNE

MORNING PRAYER

AUTHOR UNKNOWN

Into the hands of Thy blessed protection and unspeakable mercy, O Lord, I commend this day my soul and my body, with all the faculties, powers, and actions of them both, beseeching Thee to be ever with me, to direct, sanctify, and govern me in the ways of Thy laws and in the works of Thy commandments; that, through Thy most mighty protection, both here and ever, I may be preserved in body and soul to serve Thee, the only true God, through Jesus Christ our Lord. Amen.

EVENING PRAYER

ROBERT LOUIS STEVENSON

Go with each of us to rest; if any awake, temper to them the dark hours of watching. And when the day returns, return to us, our sun and comforter, and call us up with morning faces and with morning hearts, eager to labour, eager to be happy if happiness should be our portion, and if the day be marked for sorrow, strong to endure it.

A Prayer for Joy

AUTHOR UNKNOWN

Almighty God, grant that I may awake to the joy of this day, finding gladness in all its toil and difficulty and in its pleasure and success, in all its failures and sorrow; teach me to throw open the windows of my life, that I may look always away from myself and behold the need of the world. Give me the will and strength to bring the gift of Thy gladness to others of Thy children, that with them I may stand to bear the burden and heat of the day and offer Thee the praise of work well done, through Jesus Christ our Lord. Amen.

A Daily Prayer

HENRY VAN DYKE

Grant us the knowledge that we need to solve the questions of the mind; light Thou our candle while we read, and keep our hearts from going blind; enlarge our vision to behold the wonders Thou hast wrought of old; reveal Thyself in every law, and gild the towers of truth with holy awe. Amen.

An Evening Prayer

JANE AUSTEN

We thank Thee with all our hearts for every gracious dispensation; for all the blessings that have attended our lives; for every hour of safety, health, and peace, of domestic comfort and innocent enjoyment.

We feel that we have been blessed far beyond any thing that we have deserved; and though we cannot but pray for a continuance of all these mercies, we acknowledge our unworthiness of them and implore Thee to pardon the presumption of our desires.

Keep us, O Heavenly Father, from evil this night. Bring us in safety to the beginning of another day and grant that we may rise again with every serious and religious feeling which now directs us.

May Thy mercy be extended over all mankind, bringing the ignorant to the knowledge of Thy truth, awakening the impenitent, touching the hardened. Look with compassion upon the afflicted of every condition, assuage the pangs of disease, comfort the broken in spirit.

PRAYER FOR THE PERSECUTED

MILES COVERDALE

O God, give us patience when the wicked hurt us. Oh, how impatient and angry we are when we think ourselves unjustly slandered, reviled, and hurt. Christ suffers strokes upon his cheek, the innocent for the guilty; yet we may not abide one rough word for His sake.

O Lord, grant us virtue and patience, power and strength, that we may take all adversity with good will and with a gentle mind overcome it. And if necessity and Your honour require us to speak, grant that we may do so with meekness and patience, that the truth and Your glory may be defended and our patience and steadfast continuance perceived.

Likewise the Spirit also helpeth our infirmities: for we know not what we should pray for as we ought: but the Spirit itself maketh intercession for us with groanings which cannot be uttered.

ROMANS 8:26

I rejoice at thy word, as one that findeth great spoil.

PSALM 119:162

FOR PITY AND MERCY

EUGÈNE BERSIER

You are love, and You see all the suffering, injustice, and misery, which reign in this world. Have pity, we implore You, on the work of Your hands. Look mercifully on the poor, the oppressed, and all who are heavy laden with error, labour, and sorrow. Fill our hearts with deep compassion for those who suffer, and hasten the coming of Your kingdom of justice and truth.

A PRAYER OF PETITION

EDWARD BOUVERI PUSEY

O Lord Jesus Christ, when on earth you were ever occupied about your Father's business; grant that we may not grow weary in well-doing. Give us grace to do all in Your name; be the beginning and the end of all, the Pattern whom we follow, the Redeemer in whom we trust, the Master whom we serve, the Friend to whom we look for sympathy.

Bring us at last into the eternal presence, where with the Father and the Holy Ghost You live and reign for ever. Amen.

PERSEVERANCE

SIR FRANCIS DRAKE

O Lord God, when Thou givest to Thy servants to endeavor any great matter, grant us also to know that it is not the beginning but the continuing of the same, until it be thoroughly finished, which yieldeth the true glory; through Him that for the finishing of Thy work laid down His life, our Redeemer, Jesus Christ.

PRAYER FOR OUR WORK

THOMAS ARNOLD

Let Thy blessing, O Lord, rest upon our work this day. Teach us to seek after truth, and enable us to attain it; but grant that as we increase in the knowledge of earthly things, we may grow in the knowledge of Thee, whom to know is life eternal; through Jesus Christ our Lord.

A Mother's Prayer

AUTHOR UNKNOWN

My God, to Thee my heart is uplifted, as I commend unto Thy protecting care those dearest on earth to me. Guard well my husband and my children, all the members of my family, and all the inmates of my home. Preserve them from sorrow and misfortune; hold suffering and ailment far from us, that we may fear neither the dangers of the day nor the terrors of the night.

May Thy providence hold watch and ward over us in the performance of our daily duties. Give me Thine aid in controlling vain promptings within me so that I may rule my life with virtue and uprightness before Thee. Preserve me from idleness and foolish yearning for worldly pleasure; teach me that in my home I shall find my purest joys, my most pleasurable emotions in acts of motherly devotion, self-forgetfulness, and simplicity.

Bless me and those I love with health and cheerfulness; shield us all from temptation and sin. Let us find favor and regard in Thine eyes and in the eyes of all good men. Sustain and strengthen my husband in his daily labors; give him courage and endurance. Preserve forever the tranquility of our happy home and the peace that dwells in our hearts. For this I beseech Thee, for this have I set my heart before Thee, Lord, my rock and my Redeemer. Amen.

If you pray for another, you will be helped yourself.

AUTHOR UNKNOWN

KEEP ALL MY CHILDREN

Lord, keep all my children free to love.
Never let the slightest shade of suspicion
Shadow any heart. Help each to think the best
Of every other. Through all the chances and
Changes of life, hold all together in tender love.

Let nothing quench love. Let nothing cool it.
Keep every thread of the gold cord unbroken,
Unweakened, even unto the end. O my Lord,
Thou Loving One, keep my beloved close
Together in Thy love for ever.

AMY CARMICHAEL

PRAYER FOR OUR CHILDREN

Bless my children with healthful bodies,
With good understandings,
With the graces and gifts of Thy Spirit,
With sweet dispositions and holy habits;

And sanctify them throughout
In their bodies and souls and spirits,
And keep them unblamable
To the coming of the Lord Jesus.

JEREMY TAYLOR

PROTECT AND GUIDE

JEAN A. ZIGLAR

Dear Lord, thank You for each of our children. They are so precious to us. Watch over and protect them as they mature and grow closer to You. Help them to realize that You are all they need to live a fulfilled life here on earth.

Let your light shine through us for them to see so that they may know that You are the truth and the way. Thank You, Lord.

PRAYER FOR OUR CHILDREN

Great God, with heart and tongue
   To Thee aloud we pray,
That all our children, while they're young,
   May walk in wisdom's way.

Now in their early days,
   Teach them Thy will to know;
O God, Thy sanctifying grace
   On every heart bestow.

Make their defenseless youth
   The object of Thy care;
Cause them to choose the way of truth
   And flee from every snare.

Their hearts to folly prone,
   Renew by power divine;
Unite them to Thyself alone,
   And make them wholly Thine.

AUTHOR UNKNOWN

TURNING CHILDREN'S CARES OVER TO GOD

RUTH BELL GRAHAM

Lord, I think it is harder to turn the worries and cares of my children over to You than my own. For through the years, as I have grown in faith, I have learned that You are merciful and kind.

Not one time have You failed me, Lord—why do I fear You will fail mine?

*Father, may wisdom,
peace, and courage be in
my child's heart.*

BARBARA BUSH

Prayer is the central avenue God uses to transform us.

RICHARD J. FOSTER

PRAYER FOR FAMILY LIFE

ROBERT LOUIS STEVENSON

Lord, behold our family here assembled. We thank Thee for this place in which we dwell; for the love that unites us; for the peace accorded us this day; for the hope with which we expect on the morrow; for the health, the work, the food, and the bright skies that make our lives delightful; for our friends in all parts of the earth and our friendly helpers in this foreign isle.

Let peace abound in our small company. Amen.

PRAYER FOR FAMILY LOVE

Father,
Grant unto us true family love,
That we may belong more entirely
To those whom Thou hast given us,
Understanding each other, day by day,
More instinctively; forbearing each other,
Day by day, more patiently; growing,
Day by day, more closely into oneness
With each other.

Father,
Thou too art love: Thou knowest
The depth of pain and the height of glory
Which abide continually in love.
Make us perfect in love for these our dear ones,
As knowing that without them
We can never be made perfect in Thee.

Father,
Bring to full fruit in us Thine own nature,
That nature of humble redemptive devotion,
Which out of two responsive souls,
Can create a new heaven and a new earth,
One eternal glory of divine self-sharing.

AUTHOR UNKNOWN

BLESSED IS EVERY ONE THAT FEARETH THE LORD

Blessed is every one that feareth the LORD;
    that walketh in his ways.
For thou shalt eat the labour of thine hands;
Happy shalt thou be, and it shall be well
    with thee.
Thy wife shall be as a fruitful vine
    by the sides of thine house:
    thy children like olive plants
    round about thy table.
Behold, that thus shall the man be blessed
    that feareth the LORD.
The LORD shall bless thee out of Zion:
    and thou shalt see the good of Jerusalem
    all the days of thy life.
Yea, thou shalt see thy children's children,
    and peace upon Israel.
PSALM 128

It is impossible to overstate the need for prayer in the fabric of family life.

JAMES C. DOBSON

UNTO THEE, O GOD, DO WE GIVE THANKS

Unto thee, O God, do we give thanks,
    unto thee do we give thanks:
    for that thy name is near
    thy wondrous works declare.
When I shall receive the congregation
    I will judge uprightly.
The earth and all the inhabitants thereof are dissolved:
    I bear up the pillars of it. *Selah*.

I said unto the fools, Deal not foolishly:
    and to the wicked, Lift not up the horn:
Lift not up your horn on high: speak not with a stiff neck.

For promotion cometh neither from the east,
    nor from the west, nor from the south.
But God is the judge: he putteth down one,
    and setteth up another.
For in the hand of the LORD there is a cup,
    and the wine is red; it is full of mixture;
    and he poureth out of the same:
    but the dregs thereof, all the wicked of the earth
    shall wring them out, and drink them.

But I will declare for ever; I will sing praises
    to the God of Jacob.
All the horns of the wicked also will I cut off;
    but the horns of the righteous shall be exalted.
PSALM 75

THE SEVENTY-FIFTH PSALM

Thee, God, O Thee, we sing, we celebrate:
Thy acts with wonder who but doth relate?
    So kindly nigh Thy name our need attendeth.
Sure I, when once the charge I undergo
Of this assembly, will not fail to show
    My judgments such as justest rule commendeth.

The people loose, the land I shaken find:
This will I firmly prop, that straitly bind;
    And then denounce my uncontrolled pleasure:
Brag not you braggarts; you your saucy horn
Lift not, lewd mates: no more with heaven's scorn
    Dance on in words your old repining measure.

Where sun first shows or last enshades his light
Divides the day or pricks the midst of night;
    Seek not the fountain whence preferment springeth.
God's only fixed course that all doth sway,
Limits dishonors night and honors day;
    The king his crown, the slave his fetters bringeth.

A troubled cup is in Jehovah's hand,
Where wine and winy lees compounded stand,
    Which frankly filled, as freely He bestoweth;
Yet for their draught ungodly men doth give,
Gives all (not one except) that lewdly live,
    Only what from the dregs by wringing floweth.

And I, secure, shall spend my happy times
In my, though lowly, never-dying rhymes,
    Singing with praise the God that Jacob loveth.
My princely care shall crop ill-doers low,
In glory plant, and make with glory grow
    Who right approves, and doth what right approveth.

MARY SIDNEY HERBERT

THANKS FOR YOUR CREATION

WALTER RAUSCHENBUSH

O God, we thank You for this earth, our home; for the wide sky and the blessed sun; for the salt sea and the running water; for the everlasting hills and the never resting winds; for trees and the common grass underfoot.

We thank You for our senses by which we hear the songs of birds, and see the splendour of the summer fields and taste of the autumn fruits and rejoice in the feel of the snow and smell the breath of the spring.

Grant us a heart wide open to all this beauty; and save our souls from being so blind that we pass unseeing when even the common thornbush is aflame with Your glory, O God our creator, who lives and reigns forever and ever. Amen.

I THANK YOU GOD

i thank You God for most this amazing
day: for the leaping greenly spirits of trees
and a blue true dream of sky; and for everything
which is natural which is infinite which is yes

(i who have died am alive again today,
and this is the sun's birthday; this is the birth
day of life and of love and wings: and of the gay
great happening illimitable earth)

how should tasting touching hearing seeing
breathing any—lifted from the no
of all nothing—human merely being
doubt unimaginable You?

(now the ears of my ears awake and
now the eyes of my eyes are opened)
E. E. CUMMINGS

*Thank you, Lord, for the sheer joy of wanting
to get up and help the world go around.*
ROXIE GIBSON

WE THANK THEE

For mother-love and father-care,
For brothers strong and sisters fair,
For love at home and here each day,
For guidance lest we go astray,
    Father in Heaven, we thank Thee.

For this new morning with its light,
For rest and shelter of the night,
For health and food, for love and friends,
For everything His goodness sends,
    Father in Heaven, we thank Thee.

For flowers that bloom about our feet,
For tender grass, so fresh, so sweet,
For song of bird and hum of bee,
For all things fair we hear or see,
    Father in Heaven, we thank Thee.

For blue of stream and blue of sky,
For pleasant shade of branches high,
For fragrant air and cooling breeze,
For beauty of the blooming trees,
    Father in Heaven, we thank Thee.
RALPH WALDO EMERSON

PRAYER FOR OUR FRIENDS

JEREMY TAYLOR

Be pleased, O Lord, to remember my friends, all that have prayed for me, and all that have done me good. Do Thou good to them, and return all their kindness double into their own bosom, rewarding them with blessings and sanctifying them with Thy graces and bringing them to glory.

Thank You for making all things beautiful in their time and for putting eternity into our hearts.

AUTHOR UNKNOWN

ALL PEOPLE THAT ON EARTH DO DWELL

All people that on earth do dwell,
    Sing to the Lord with cheerful voice.
Him serve with fear; His praise forth tell.
    Come ye before Him and rejoice.

Know that the Lord is God indeed;
    Without our aid He did us make.
We are His folk; He doth us feed,
    And for His sheep He doth us take.

Oh enter then His gates with praise;
    Approach with joy His courts unto.
Praise, laud, and bless His Name always
    For it is seemly so to do.

For why? The Lord our God is good;
    His mercy is for ever sure.
His truth at all times firmly stood,
    And shall from age to age endure.

WILLIAM KETHE

Prayer for Protection

Edward Diby

Visit, we beseech Thee, most gracious Father, this family and household with Thy protection. Let Thy blessing descend and rest on all that belong to it, as well absent as present. Grant us and them whatever may be expedient or profitable for our bodies or our souls. Guide us by Thy good providence here, and hereafter bring us all to Thy glory; through Jesus Christ our Lord. Amen.

Paul's Prayer

Ephesians 3:14–21

For this cause I bow my knees unto the Father of our Lord Jesus Christ, of whom the whole family in heaven and earth is named, that he would grant you, according to the riches of his glory, to be strengthened with might by his Spirit in the inner man; that Christ may dwell in your hearts by faith; that ye, being rooted and grounded in love, may be able to comprehend with all saints what is the breadth, and length, and depth, and height; and to know the love of Christ, which passeth knowledge, that ye might be filled with all the fullness of God.

Now unto him that is able to do exceedingly abundantly above all that we ask or think, according to the power that worketh in us, unto him be glory in the church by Christ Jesus throughout all ages, world without end. Amen.

Prayer for Parents

Desiderius Erasmus

O Lord God, whose will it is that, next to Yourself, we should hold our parents in highest honour; it is not the least of our duties to beseech Your goodness towards them.

Preserve, I pray, my parents and home in the love of Your religion and in health of body and mind. Grant that through me no sorrow may befall them; and finally, as they are kind to me, so may You be to them, O supreme Father of all.

God be merciful unto us, and bless us.

PSALM 67:1

PRAYER FOR GRANDPARENTS

Most loving God,
We ask Your blessing
Upon our grandparents.
They connect us
With the generations before us
And remind us of our responsibility
To the generations to come,
For whom we shall be their ancestors.

Bless our grandparents
With loving families, with good health,
With compassionate and tender friends.
Grant us the wisdom to give unto them
Honor, respect, and love
That their days may be a blessing.
In the name of Christ we pray.
Amen.

VIENNA COBB ANDERSON

77

GOD BE MERCIFUL

God be merciful unto us, and bless us;
    and cause his face to shine upon us; *Selah*.

That thy way may be known upon earth,
    thy saving health among all nations.
Let the people praise thee, O God;
    let all the people praise thee.
O let the nations be glad and sing for joy:
    for thou shalt judge the people righteously,
    and govern the nations upon earth. *Selah*.

Let the people praise thee, O God;
    let all the people praise thee.
Then shall the earth yield her increase;
    and God, even our own God, shall bless us.
God shall bless us; and all the ends of the earth
    shall fear him.

PSALM 67

THE SIXTY-SEVENTH PSALM

Show us Thy mercy, Lord, and grace divine;
Turn Thy bright face, that it on us may shine,
That all the men on earth enlightened so,
Their own salvation and Thy ways may know.

Oh let Thy people praise Thy blessed name,
And let all tongues and nations do the same,
And let all mortal men rejoice in this,
That God their judge and just His judgment is.

Oh let Thy people praise Thy blessed name,
And let all tongues and nations do the same,
Then shall the earth bring forth a rich increase,
And God shall bless us with a fruitful peace;

Even God shall bless us and His holy fear
Possess the hearts of all men everywhere.

JOHN DAVIES

THINK THROUGH ME

Think through me, thoughts of God,
My Father, quiet me,
Till in Thy holy presence, hushed,
I think Thy thoughts with Thee.

Think through me, thoughts of God,
That always, everywhere,
The stream that through my being flows,
May homeward pass in prayer.

Think through me, thoughts of God,
And let my own thoughts be
Lost like the sand-pools on the shore
Of the eternal sea.

AMY CARMICHAEL

PRAYER FOR GOD'S PEOPLE

HANDLEY MOULE

The blessing of the Lord rest and remain upon all His people, in every land, of every tongue; the Lord meet in mercy all that seek Him; the Lord comfort all who suffer and mourn; the Lord hasten His coming and give us, His people, the blessing of peace.

I will bless the LORD at all times: his praise shall continually be in my mouth.

PSALM 34:1

79

Prayer for This Land

William Laud

Lord, bless this kingdom, we beseech Thee, that religion and virtue may increase amongst us, that there may be peace within the gates and plenty within the palaces of it.

In peace, we beseech Thee, so preserve it, that it corrupt not; in war so defend it, that it suffer not; in plenty so order it, that it riot not; in want so pacify and moderate it, that it may patiently and peaceably seek Thee, the only full supply both of men and state, that so it may continue a place and a people to do Thee service to the end of time.

Bless Us with Content

O Thou, who kindly doth provide
For ev'ry creature's want,
We bless the God of nature wide
For all Thy goodness lent.

And if it please Thee, heavenly Guide,
May never worse be sent;
But, whether granted or denied,
Lord, bless us with content.

Robert Burns

Prayer for Those Who Serve

Peter Marshall

Lord Jesus, bless all who serve us, who have dedicated their lives to the ministry of others: all the teachers of our schools who labor so patiently with so little appreciation; all who wait upon the public, the clerks in the stores who have to accept criticism, complaints, bad manners, selfishness at the hands of a thoughtless public. Bless the mailman, the drivers of streetcars and buses who must listen to people who lose their tempers.

Bless every humble soul who, in these days of stress and strain, preaches sermons without words. In the name of Him who called us to be the servants of all. Amen.

A Blessing

THE BOOK OF COMMON PRAYER

Almighty God, whose loving hand hath given us all that we possess, give us also grace to honor Thee with our substance, remembering the account we must one day give as faithful stewards of Thy bounty; for the sake of Jesus Christ our Lord. Amen.

GIVE US THIS DAY OUR DAILY BREAD   THANKSGIVING

In giving thanks, we are blessed.
AUTHOR UNKNOWN

HARVEST BLESSING

O God Our Father,
The foundation of all goodness,
Who has been gracious to us
Not only in the year that is past
But throughout all the years of our lives,
We give You thanks for Your loving kindness
Which has filled our days
And brought us to this time and place.
JOHN WESLEY

PRAYER OF THANKSGIVING

Blessed are You, Lord.
You have fed us from our earliest days;
You give food to every living creature.
Fill our hearts with joy and delight.
Let us always have enough
And something to spare for works of mercy
In honor of Christ Jesus, our Lord.
Through Him may glory, honor, and power
Be Yours forever.
AUTHOR UNKNOWN

FOR THE LORD THY GOD

For the LORD thy God bringeth thee into a good land,
    a land of brooks of water,
    of fountains and depths that spring
    out of valleys and hills;
A land of wheat, and barley, and vines,
    and fig trees, and pomegranates;
    a land of oil olive, and honey;
A land wherein thou shalt eat bread without scarceness,
    thou shalt not lack any thing in it;
    a land whose stones are iron,
    and out of whose hills thou mayest dig brass.
When thou hast eaten and art full,
    then thou shalt bless the LORD thy God
    for the good land which he hath given thee.

DEUTERONOMY 8:7–10

FOR PEACE AT TABLE

Lord Christ, we pray Thy mercy on our table spread;
And what Thy gentle hands have given Thy men,
Let it by Thee be blessed: whate'er we have
Came from Thy lavish heart and gentle hand;
And all that's good is Thine, for Thou art good.
And ye that eat, give thanks for it to Christ,
And let the words ye utter be only peace,
For Christ loves peace: it was Himself that said,
"Peace I give unto you, my peace I leave with you."
Grant that our own may be a generous hand
Breaking the bread for all poor men, sharing the food.
Christ shall receive the bread thou givest His poor,
And shall not tarry to give thee reward.

ALCUIN OF YORK

GOD, BLESS THIS FOOD

God, who invites us always
    to spiritual delights,
Give blessing over Your gifts
    so that we might deserve
To partake in the blessed things
    which ought to be added
    to Your name.
Let Your gifts refresh us, Lord,
    and let Your grace comfort us.

AUTHOR UNKNOWN

A FARM-TABLE BLESSING

The blessing of God rest upon all those who
    have been kind to us,
    have cared for us,
    have worked for us,
    have served us,
    and have shared our bread with us
    at this table.

AUTHOR UNKNOWN

HARVEST THANKSGIVING

Lord of the harvest, hear
    Thy needy servants' cry;
Answer our faith's effectual prayer,
    And all our wants supply.

On Thee we humbly wait;
    Our wants are in Thy view.
The harvest truly, Lord, is great,
    The laborers are few.

CHARLES WESLEY

BLESS ME

JAKOB BÖEHME

Bless me and all I am about and do this day with the blessing of Thy love and mercy. Continue Thy grace and love in Jesus Christ upon me, and give me a mind cheerfully to follow Thy leadings and execute Thine appointment. Let Thy Holy Spirit guide me in my beginning and my progress on to my last end.

Bless Our Day, O God

Matthew Henry

O Lord, lift up the light of Your countenance upon us; let Your peace rule in our hearts, and may it be our strength and our song in the house of our pilgrimage. We commit ourselves to Your care and keeping; let Your grace be mighty in us and sufficient in us for all the duties of the day.

Keep us from sin. Give us rule over our spirits, and guard us from speaking unadvisedly with our lips. May we live together in holy love and peace, and do command Your blessing upon us, even life for evermore. Amen.

Make Me a Blessing

James Dillet Freeman

Make me a blessing, Lord. Help me to assist those needing help, to be a blessing to my fellowmen. Instruct me when to speak and when to hold my speech, when to be bold in giving and when to withhold; and if I have not strength enough, then give me strength.

Lord, make me love myself and be tender toward all others. Let there be outpoured on me the gentleness to bless all who have need of gentleness. Give me a word, a touch to fill the lonely life, faith for the ill, and courage to keep hearts up though my own is feeling just as low. When men have bitter things to meet and quail and would accept defeat, then let me lift their eyes to see the vision of Thy victory. Help me to help; help me to give the wisdom and the will to live.

Father, glorify thy name.
John 12:28

Bless Our Workday

Sid G. Hedges

O Lord, we beseech Thee to bless and prosper us gathered here together this day. Grant us reasonableness in all our dealings with each other. Make us large-hearted in helping and generous in criticizing. Keep us from unkind words and unkind silences. Make us quick to understand the needs and feelings of others, and grant that, living in the brightness of Thy presence, we may bring Thy sunshine into cloudy places, like true followers of Jesus Christ our Lord.

DEAR LORD! KIND LORD!

Dear Lord! Kind Lord!
    Gracious Lord! I pray
Thou wilt look on all I love
    Tenderly today.

Weed their hearts of weariness;
    Scatter every care
Down a wake of angel-wings
    Winnowing the air.

And with all the needy
    Oh divide, I pray,
This vast treasure of content
    That is mine today.

JAMES WHITCOMB RILEY

*Blessings are upon
the head of the just.*

PROVERBS 10:6

THE BEATITUDES

Blessed are the poor in spirit:
    for theirs is the kingdom of heaven.
Blessed are they that mourn:
    for they shall be comforted.
Blessed are the meek:
    for they shall inherit the earth.
Blessed are they which do hunger
    and thirst after righteousness:
    for they shall be filled.
Blessed are the merciful:
    for they shall obtain mercy.
Blessed are the pure in heart:
    for they shall see God.
Blessed are the peacemakers:
    for they shall be called the children of God.
Blessed are they which are persecuted
    for righteousness' sake:
    for theirs is the kingdom of heaven.
Blessed are ye, when men shall revile you,
    and persecute you, and shall say all manner of evil
    against you falsely, for my sake.

MATTHEW 5:3–11

BLESSED ART THOU, O LORD

LANCELOT ANDREWES

Blessed art Thou, O Lord, who has created and brought me forth into this life.

To Thee, O God of my fathers, I give thanks; Thee I praise, who hast in some measure endured me with wisdom and might and hast made known unto me that which I desired of Thee and hast made known to me the King's matter; who hast made me the work of Thine hands, the price of Thy blood, the image of Thy countenance, the servant of Thy purchase, the seal of Thy name, the child of Thy adoption, a temple of Thy spirit, a member of Thy church.

Our merciful God, reward all of them in Your own way.

SAINT CYRIL

To all else Thou hast given us,
O Lord, we ask for but one thing more:
Give us grateful hearts.

GEORGE HERBERT

O Lord, that lends me life,
Lend me a heart replete with thankfulness.

WILLIAM SHAKESPEARE

God, of Your goodness, give me Yourself,
for You are sufficient for me. I cannot
properly ask anything less, to be worthy of
You. If I were to ask less, I should always
be in want. In You alone do I have all.

JULIAN OF NORWICH

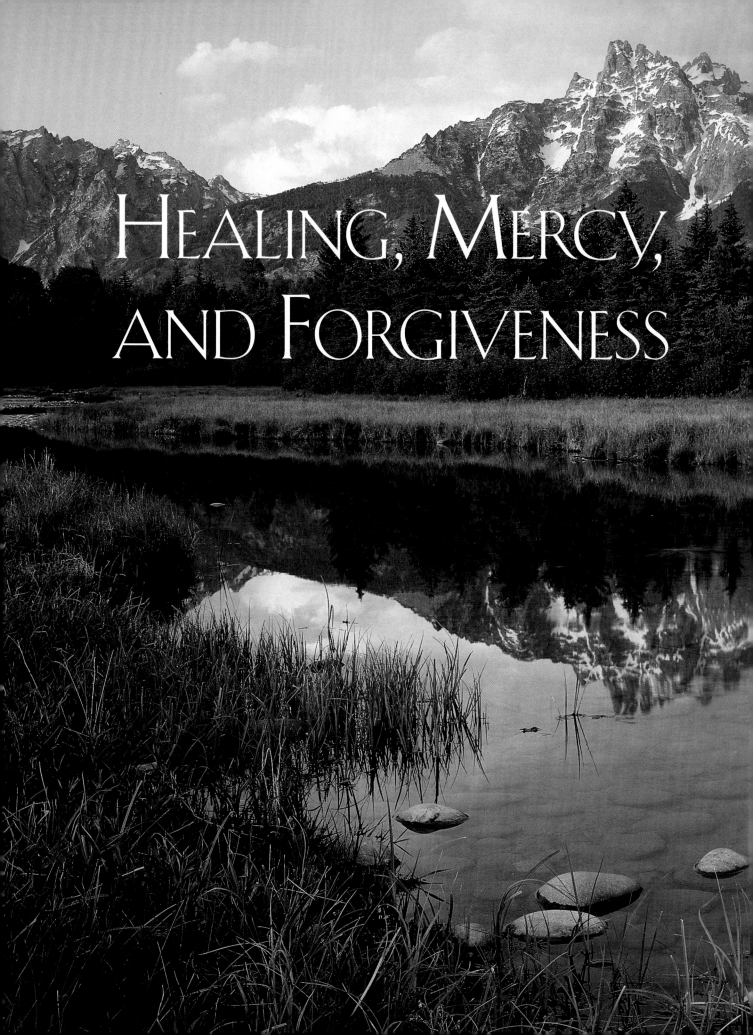

HEALING, MERCY, AND FORGIVENESS

CHAPTER FOUR

And forgive us our debts, as we forgive our debtors . . .

Help me, O God, to be a good and a true friend: to be always
loyal and never to let my friends down. This I ask for the sake of Him
who is the greatest and truest of all friends, for Jesus' sake. Amen.
WILLIAM BARCLAY

SUPPLICATIONS FOR MERCY

JOHN DONNE

O Eternal and most gracious God, who Thou beest ever infinite yet enlargest Thyself by the number of our prayers, and takest our often petitions to Thee to be an addition to Thy glory and Thy greatness, as ever upon all occasions, so now, my God, I come to Thy majesty with two prayers, two supplications.

I have meditated upon the jealousy which Thou hast of Thine own honour, nearer to the nature of a scorn to Thee, than to see Thy pardon, and receive the seals of reconciliation to Thee, and to return to that sin for which I needed and had Thy pardon before. Know that this comes too near to making Thy holy ordinances, Thy word, Thy sacraments, Thy seals, Thy grace, instruments of my spiritual fornications.

Since therefore Thy correction hath brought me to such a participation of Thyself (Thyself, O my God, cannot be parted), to such an entire possession of Thee, as that I durst deliver myself over to Thee this minute, if this minute Thou wouldst accept my dissolution, preserve me, O my God, the God of constancy and perseverance, in this state, from all relapses into those sins which have induced Thy former judgements upon me.

But because, by too lamentable experience, I know how slippery my customs of sin have made my ways of sin, I presume to add this petition too, that if my infirmity overtake me, Thou forsake me not. Say to my soul, "My son, thou hast sinned, do so no more;" but say also, that though I do, Thy spirit of remorse and compunction shall never depart from me.

Thy holy apostle, Saint Paul, was shipwrecked thrice, and yet still saved. Though the rocks and the sands the heights and the shallows, the prosperity and the adversity of this world, do diversely threaten me, though mine own leaks endanger me; yet, O God, let me never put myself aboard with Hymenaeus, nor make a shipwreck of faith and a good conscience, and then Thy long-lived, Thy everlasting mercy, will visit me, though that which I most earnestly pray against, should fall upon me: a relapse into those sins which I have truly repented, and Thou hast fully pardoned.

Pastorate Prayer for Healing

Peter Marshall

There are loved ones, O Lord, for whom we pray, and the prayers are even now being whispered before the throne of grace. We ask for Thy help without any hesitation, knowing that Thou are disposed to give even before we ask.

We thank Thee for askings that have been received and prayers that have been answered. We are so glad that by Thy grace and mercy broken bones have been mended, weak and struggling hearts have been made strong. We thank Thee that pain has been removed; the sick have so often been made well.

Hear us as we pray now for some who need stronger hearts. Thou art the great Doctor who can do it. Wilt Thou strengthen the hearts of them who we name even now?

And now grant to us that spiritual perception and faith that, having asked, reaches out to accept Thy good gifts. Help us to keep our eyes on Thee and not on symptoms. And grant, in Thine own time and Thine own way, a complete return to that health and strength which is Thy perfect will for Thy children. In Thy strength, who art the same, yesterday, today, and forever, we pray. Amen.

For he had healed many; insomuch that they pressed upon him for to touch him.

MARK 3:10

A Prayer for Healing

Aelred of Rievaulx

Lord, just as day declines to evening, so often after some little pleasure my heart declines into depression. Everything seems dull; every action feels like a burden. If anyone speaks, I scarcely listen. If anyone knocks, I scarcely hear. My heart is as hard as flint.

Then I go out into the field to meditate, to read the holy Scriptures; and I write down my deepest thoughts in a letter to You. And suddenly Your grace, dear Jesus, shatters the darkness with daylight, lifts the burden, relieves the tension.

Soon tears follow sighs, and heavenly joy floods over me with the tears.

UNITY

Behold, how good and how pleasant
    it is for brethren to dwell
      together in unity!
It is like the precious ointment
    upon the head, that ran down
      upon the beard, even Aaron's beard:
      that went down to the skirts
    of his garments;
As the dew of Hermon,
    and as the dew that descended
      upon the mountains of Zion:
      for there the LORD commanded
    the blessing, even life for evermore.

PSALM 133

THE HUNDRED THIRTY-THIRD PSALM

It's so good, the turn of a season
people living for a moment as equals
secure in the human family

as sweet as spring rain
making the beard silky
Aaron's beard

his robes sparkle
rich with heaven's simple jewels
like the crown of dew

on Lebanon's Mt. Hermon
shared equally on the hills of Israel

where the Lord graces our eyes
fresh from reborn wonder
as if we'd live forever.

DAVID ROSENBERG

IN A TIME OF DISCOURAGEMENT

God, help me now to know and to remember,
Though there are moments when
All wings that soar into the blue are folded,
There will be flight again!

In hours when buds look much too hard for bursting
A fragile-petaled way,
Give me then patient knowledge of the coming
Of leaf and blossom spray.

God, when the day seems like a level wasteland,
Teach me that widest skies
Stretch over the most arid, treeless places—
Help me to lift mine eyes!

VIOLET ALLEYN STOREY

A Daily Prayer

JOHN BAILLIE

Eternal Father of my soul, let my first thought today be of Thee; let my first impulse be to worship Thee; let my first speech be Thy name; let my first action be to kneel before Thee in prayer.

And Jesus saith unto him, I will come and heal him.
MATTHEW 8:7

Between the humble and contrite heart and the majesty of heaven, there are no barriers; the only password is prayer.
HOSEA BALLOU

PRAYER FOR WHOLENESS

Dear Lord, let me drink from
    You so deeply that I, too,
    may share
The peace, beauty, and contentment
    that others have found there.
Let me, too, stand on Your
    highest mountaintop
So Your love engulfs me, so lost
    I am not.
Let me drink from Your never-ending
    well of healing waters and
    hold my head high,
Making me whole and at peace,
    no long questioning or
    asking why.
Just fill me with Your goodness
    that I, too, may be refreshed anew
By letting me find the wonderment
    of receiving and accepting You.
MARY JANE COOK

Pray not for crutches but for wings.

PHILLIPS BROOKS

PRAYER FOR HEALING

At even, ere the sun had set,
The sick, O Lord, around Thee lay;
Oh in what diverse pains they met!
Oh with what joy they went away!

Once more 'tis eventide, and we
Oppressed by various ills draw near:
What if Thy form we cannot see?
We know and feel that Thou art here.

Thy touch has still its ancient power;
No word from Thee can fruitless fall;
Hear, in this solemn evening hour,
And in Thy mercy heal us all.
HENRY TWELLS

GOD'S RICH MERCY

But God, who is rich in mercy,
    for his great love wherewith he loved us,
And hath raised us up together, and made us
    sit together in heavenly places in Christ Jesus:
That in the ages to come he might show the
    exceeding riches of his grace.
EPHESIANS 2:4, 6–7

Prayer of a Penitent Heart

John Chrysostom

I am not worthy, Master and Lord, that Thou shouldest come beneath the roof of my soul: yet, since Thou in Thy love toward all men, dost wish to dwell in me, in boldness I come.

Thou commandest, open the gates—which thou alone hast forged. And Thou wilt come in with love toward all men, as is Thy nature; Thou wilt come in and enlighten my darkened reasoning.

I believe that Thou wilt do this: for Thou didst not send away the harlot who came to Thee with tears; nor cast out the repenting publican; nor reject the thief who acknowledged Thy kingdom; nor forsake the repentant persecutor, a yet greater act; but all of those who came to Thee in repentance didst Thou count in the band of Thy friends, who alone abidest blessed forever, now, and until the endless ages. Amen.

*O Lord, forgive me for what
I have been, sanctify what I am,
and order what I shall be.*

FRANK MacNUTT

Be Ye Therefore Merciful

And as ye would that men should do to you,
    do ye also to them likewise.
But love ye your enemies, and do good,
    and lend, hoping for nothing again;
    and your reward shall be great,
    and ye shall be the children of the Highest:
    for he is kind unto the unthankful and to the evil.
Be ye therefore merciful,
    as your Father also is merciful.
LUKE 6:31, 35–36

My Daily Prayer

Bless me, heavenly Father,
Forgive my erring ways,
Grant me strength to serve Thee,
Put purpose in my days.

Give me understanding,
Enough to make me kind,
So I may judge all people
With my heart and not my mind.

And teach me to be patient
In everything I do,
Content to trust Your wisdom
And to follow after You.

And help me when I falter,
And hear me when I pray,
And receive me in Thy kingdom,
To dwell with Thee some day.
Amen.

HELEN STEINER RICE

Because of Thy Great Bounty

Because I have been given much,
I, too, must give:
Because of Thy great bounty, Lord,
Each day I live
I shall divide my gifts from Thee
With every brother that I see
Who has the need of help from me.

Because I have been sheltered, fed,
By Thy good care,
I cannot see another's lack
And I not share
My glowing fire, my loaf of bread,
My roof's safe shelter overhead,
That he, too, may be comforted.

Because love has been lavished so
Upon me, Lord,
A wealth I know that was not meant
For me to hoard,
I shall give love to those in need,
Shall show that love by word and deed,
Thus shall my thanks be thanks indeed.

GRACE NOLL CROWELL

We do pray for mercy . . .

WILLIAM SHAKESPEARE

PRAYER FOR MERCY

SAINT JEROME

Show me, O Lord, in Your mercy, and delight my heart with it. Let me find You whom I so longingly seek. See, here is the man whom the robbers seized, mishandled, and left half dead on the road to Jericho. O kind-hearted Samaritan, come to my aid!

I am the sheep who wandered into the wilderness—seek after me, and bring me home again to Your fold. Do with me what You will, that I may stay by You all the days of my life and praise You with all those who are with You in heaven for all eternity.

Prayer for Peace and Mercy

Gilbert of Hoyland

When we see dark gray clouds forming in the sky, we fear a mighty storm. In the same way when we seek the darkness of our sin, we fear the storm of Your wrath. But just as in truth rain brings new life to the earth, so You rain down mercy on our sinful souls, bringing forgiveness and peace.

Be to us always like a mighty storm, raining down upon us the abundant waters of Your mercy. Amen.

Do Thou for Me

Do Thou for me, O God the Lord,
Do Thou for me.
I need not toil to find the word
That carefully
Unfolds my prayer and offers it,
My God, to Thee.

It is enough that Thou wilt do,
And wilt not tire,
Wilt lead by cloud, all the night through
By light of fire,
Till Thou hast perfected in me
Thy heart's desire.

For my beloved I will not fear,
Love knows to do
For him, for her, from year to year,
As hitherto.
Whom my heart cherishes are dear
To Thy heart too.

O blessed be the love that bears
The burden now,
The love that frames our very prayers,
Well knowing how
To coin our gold. O God the Lord,
Do Thou, Do Thou.

Amy Carmichael

There's a Wideness in God's Mercy

There's a wideness in God's mercy
    Like the wideness of the sea;
There's a kindness in His justice,
    Which is more than liberty.
There is welcome for the sinner
    And more graces for the good;
There is mercy with the Saviour;
    There is healing in His blood.

There is no place where earth's sorrows
    Are more felt than up in heaven;
There is no place where earth's failings
    Have such kindly judgment given.
There is plentiful redemption
    In the blood that has been shed;
There is joy for all the members
    In the sorrows of the Head.

For the love of God is broader
    Than the measure of man's mind;
And the heart of the Eternal
    Is most infinitely kind.
If our love were but more simple,
    We should take Him at His word;
And our lives would be all sunshine
    In the sweetness of the Lord.

Frederick William Faber

Prayer—secret, fervent, believing prayer—
lies at the root of all personal godliness.

WILLIAM CARY

A LAST PRAYER

Father, I scarcely dare to pray.
   So clear I see, now it is done,
That I have wasted half my day
   And left my work but just begun;

So clear I see that things I thought
   Were right or harmless were a sin;
So clear I see that I have sought
   Unconscious, selfish aims to win;

So clear I see that I have hurt
   The soul I might have helped to save;
That I have slothful been, inert,
   Deaf to the calls Thy leaders gave.

In outskirts of Thy kingdoms vast,
   Father, the humblest spot give me;
Set me the lowliest task Thou hast:
   Let me repentant work for Thee!

HELEN HUNT JACKSON

WALK IN THE WAY OF LOVE

GERTRUDE MORE

O My God, let me walk in the way of love which knoweth not how to seek self in anything whatsoever. Let this love wholly possess my soul and heart which, I beseech Thee, may live and move only in and out of a pure sincere love for Thee. Oh! That Thy pure love were so grounded and established in my heart that I might sigh and suffer without ceasing after Thee, and be able in strength of this Thy love to live without all comfort and consolation, human or divine.

O Lord, give this love into my soul, that I may never more live nor breathe but out of a most pure love of Thee, my All and my only Good. Let me love Thee for Thyself, and nothing else but in and for Thee. Let me love nothing instead of Thee, for to give all for love is a most sweet bargain.

Let Thy love work in and by me, and let me love Thee as Thou wouldst be loved by me. I cannot tell how much love I would have of Thee, because I would love Thee beyond all that can be imagined or desired by me.

Be Thou in this, as in all other things, my chooser for me, for Thou art my only choice most dear to me. The more I shall love Thee, the more will my soul desire Thee and desire to suffer for Thee.

THE UNEXPECTED

MARJORIE HOLMES

Thank you, Lord, for these unexpected moments of love.

For the times in life when suddenly we feel Your nearness uniting us with other people.

I felt it so keenly yesterday. In a small group of people—not family, not even close friends. Actually, I had never felt any real attachment for any of them, and some I thought rather dull.

But suddenly, sitting around the fire, they became dear—very dear. Qualities I hadn't noticed before became manifest: kindness, tenderness, gaiety, goodness.

You were suddenly with us, uniting us, Your children. Revealing us to each other in a new dimension. Giving us understanding.

I felt my antagonism toward one of them melting, giving way to joy. A new awareness of another came to me; I saw charm, a loveliness unsensed before.

And as my new-sensed love flowed out to them I felt their love encompassing me. We were brothers and sisters all, needing and wanting each other. We were Your children together around the hearthfire of life. We were Your family.

SHOW US THY MERCY

Show us thy mercy, O LORD,
    and grant us thy salvation.
I will hear what God the LORD will speak:
    for he will speak peace unto his people,
    and to his saints: but let them not turn
    again to folly.
Surely his salvation is nigh them that fear him;
    that glory may dwell in our land.
Mercy and truth are met together;
    righteousness and peace have kissed each other.
Truth shall spring out of the earth;
    and righteousness shall look down from heaven.
Yea, the LORD shall give that which is good;
    and our land shall yield her increase.
Righteousness shall go before him;
    and shall set us in the way of his steps.
PSALM 85:7–13

Prayer is exhaling the spirit of man
and inhaling the spirit of God.

EDWIN KEITH

Prayer for a Nation at War

Abraham Lincoln

Grant, O merciful God, that with malice toward none, with charity to all, with firmness in the right as Thou givest us to see the right, we may strive to finish the work we are in: to bind up the nation's wounds; to care for him who shall have borne the battle and for his widow and his orphan; to do all which may achieve and cherish a just and lasting peace among ourselves and with all nations. Amen.

Prayer for Unity

Philip Melanchthon

To You, O Son of God, Lord Jesus Christ, as You pray to the eternal Father, we pray, make us one in Him. Lighten our personal distress and that of our society. Receive us into the fellowship of those who believe. Turn our hearts, O Christ, to everlasting truth and healing harmony. Amen.

Prayer for Pardon

Thomas à Kempis

I offer up unto Thee my prayers and intercessions, for those especially who have in any matter hurt, grieved, or found fault with me or who have done me any damage or displeasure; for all those also whom, at any time, I have vexed, troubled, burdened, and scandalized, by words or deeds, knowingly or in ignorance: that Thou wouldst grant us all equally pardon for our sins and for our offenses against each other. Take away from our hearts, O Lord, all suspiciousness, indignation, wrath, and contention, and whatsoever may hurt charity, and lessen brotherly love. Have mercy, O Lord, have mercy on those that crave Thy mercy, give grace unto them that stand in need thereof, and make us such that we may be worthy to enjoy Thy grace and go forward to life eternal. Amen.

A Prayer for God's Mercy

Incline us, O God,
> to think humbly of ourselves,
> to be saved only in the examination of our own conduct,
> to consider our fellow-creatures with kindness,
> and to judge of all they say and do with the charity
> which we would desire from them ourselves.
> Amen.

JANE AUSTEN

A Prayer

Of God we ask one favor,
That we may be forgiven—
For what, He is presumed to know–
The Crime, from us, is hidden–
Immured the whole of Life
Within a magic Prison
We reprimand the Happiness
That too competes with Heaven.

EMILY DICKINSON

Father of the Forsaken

ANTHONY ASHLEY COOPER

O God, the Father of the forsaken, the help of the weak, the supplier of the needy, You teach us that love towards the race of man is the bond of perfectness and the imitation of Your blessed self. Open and touch our hearts that we may see and do, both for this world and that which is to come, the things that belong to our peace. Strengthen us in the work which we have undertaken. Give us wisdom, perseverance, hope, faith, and zeal; and in Your own time and according to Your pleasure, prosper the issue; for the love of Your Son Jesus Christ. Amen.

Prayer for Forgiveness

JOHN WESLEY

Forgive them all, O Lord: our sins of omission and our sins of commission; the sins of our youth and the sins of our riper years; the sins of our souls and the sins of our bodies; our secret and our more open sins; our sins of ignorance and surprise; and our more deliberate and presumptuous sins; the sins we have done to please ourselves and the sins we have done to please others; the sins we know and remember and the sins we have forgotten; the sins we have striven to hide from others and the sins by which we have made others offend. Forgive them, O Lord; forgive them all for His sake, who died for our sins and rose for our justification, and now stands at Thy right hand to make intercession for us, Jesus Christ our Lord. Amen.

TEACH US TO LOVE

ELIZABETH GOUDGE

Lord, we thank You for all the love that has been given to us, for the love of family and friends, and above all, for Your love poured out upon us every moment of our lives in steadfast glory.

Forgive our unworthiness. Forgive the many times we have disappointed those who love us, have failed them, wearied them, saddened them. Failing them we have failed You and hurting them we have wounded our Saviour who for love's sake died for us. Lord, have mercy on us, and forgive. You do not fail those who love You. You do not change nor vary.

Teach us Your own constancy in love, Your humility, selflessness and generosity. Look in pity on our small and tarnished loving ; protect, foster, and strengthen it, that it may be less unworthy to be offered to You and to Your children. O Light of the world, teach us how to love. Amen.

Forgive, and ye shall be forgiven.
LUKE 6:37

AND FORGIVE US OUR DEBTS, AS WE FORGIVE OUR DEBTORS

PRAYER FOR PARDON

JOHN WESLEY

Pardon, O gracious Jesus, what we have been; with Your holy discipline, correct what we are. Order by Your providence what we shall be, and in the end, crown Your won gifts. Amen.

PRAYER OF SIMEON

AUTHOR UNKNOWN

O my Creator! Consume the thorns of all my offenses. Make clean my soul; make holy my mind; nail down my being in Thy fear. E'er keep watch, guard and protect me from every act and word that destroyeth the soul.

Make me holy; make me clean; set me in order. Make me comely; give me understanding; give me light. Show me as the tabernacle of Thy Spirit alone, and no more the tabernacle of sin; and make Thy slave a child of light.

For it is Thou that makest holy, and we know none other that is good but Thee; Thou art the shining brightness of souls. And to Thee, as is justly due as God and Master, we all give glory every day. Amen.

Help me, O LORD my God: O save me according to thy mercy.
PSALM 109:26

TO THE MERCIFUL FATHER

AUTHOR UNKNOWN

O merciful Father, who has given life to many and lovest all that Thou has made, give us the spirit of Thine own loving kindness that we may show mercy to all helpless creatures. Especially would we pray for those which minister to our comfort, that they may be treated with tenderness of hands, in thankfulness of heart, and that we may discover Thee, the Creator, in all created things. Amen.

Prayer is not the fruit of natural talents; it is the product of faith, of holiness, of deeply spiritual character. Men learn to pray as they learn to love.

EDWARD MCKENDREE BOUNDS

HAVE MERCY UPON ME, O GOD

PSALM 51

Have mercy upon me, O God, according to thy loving kindness: according unto the multitude of thy tender mercies blot out my transgressions. Wash me thoroughly from mine iniquity, and cleanse me from my sin. For I acknowledge my transgressions: and my sin is ever before me.

Against thee, thee only, have I sinned, and done this evil in thy sight: that thou mightest be justified when thou speakest, and be clear when thou judgest. Behold, I was shapen in iniquity; and in sin did my mother conceive me. Behold, thou desirest truth in the inward parts: and in the hidden part thou shalt make me to know wisdom.

Purge me with hyssop, and I shall be clean: wash me, and I shall be whiter than snow. Make me to hear joy and gladness; that the bones which thou hast broken may rejoice. Hide thy face from my sins, and blot out all mine iniquities. Create in me a clean heart, O God; and renew a right spirit within me.

Cast me not away from thy presence; and take not thy holy spirit from me. Restore unto me the joy of thy salvation; and uphold me with thy free spirit. Then will I teach transgressors thy ways; and sinners shall be converted unto thee.

Deliver me from bloodguiltiness, O God, thou God of my salvation: and my tongue shall sing aloud of thy righteousness.

O LORD, open thou my lips: and my mouth shall show forth thy praise. For thou desirest not sacrifice; else would I give it: thou delightest not in burnt offering. The sacrifices of God are a broken spirit: a broken and a contrite heart, O God, thou wilt not despise. Do good in thy good pleasure unto Zion: build thou the walls of Jerusalem. Then shalt thou be pleased with the sacrifices of righteousness, with burnt offering and whole burnt offering: then shall they offer bullocks upon thine altar.

DEAR LORD

Dear Lord,
Creator of the world,
Help us love one another;
Help us care for one another
As sister or as brother.

May friendship grow
From nation to nation.
Bring peace to our world,
Dear Lord of Creation.
AUTHOR UNKNOWN

MAKE ME PURE

Lord, make me pure.
Only the pure shall see Thee as Thou art,
    And shall endure.
    Lord, bring me low,
For Thou wert lowly in Thy blessed heart:
    Lord, keep me so.
    Amen.
CHRISTINA ROSSETTI

THE FIFTY-FIRST PSALM

Good God, unlock Thy magazines
Of mercy, and forgive my sins.
Oh wash and purify the foul
Pollution of my sin-stained soul,
For I confess my faults that lie
In horrid shapes before mine eye.

Against Thee only and alone
In Thy sight was this evil done,
That all men might Thy justice see
When Thou art judged for judging me.

But Thou lovest truth and shalt impart
Thy secret wisdom to my heart.
Thou shalt send joyful news, and then
My broken bones grow strong again.
Let not Thine eyes my sins survey,
But cast those cancelled debts away.

Oh make my cleansed heart a pure cell
Where a renewed spirit may dwell.
Cast me not from Thy sight, nor chase
Away from me Thy spirit of grace.

Send me Thy saving health again,
And with Thy spirit those joys maintain.
Then will I preach Thy ways and draw
Converted sinners to Thy law.

O God my God of health, unseal
My blood-shut lips, and I'll reveal
What mercies in Thy justice dwell,
And with loud voice Thy praises tell.

Could sacrifice have purged my vice,
Lord, I had brought Thee sacrifice:
But though burnt offerings are refused
Thou shalt accept the heart that's bruised;
The humbled soul, the spirit oppressed,
Lord, such oblations please Thee best.

Then will we holy vows present Thee
And peace offerings that content Thee,
And then Thine altars shall be pressed
With many a sacrificed beast.
THOMAS CAREW

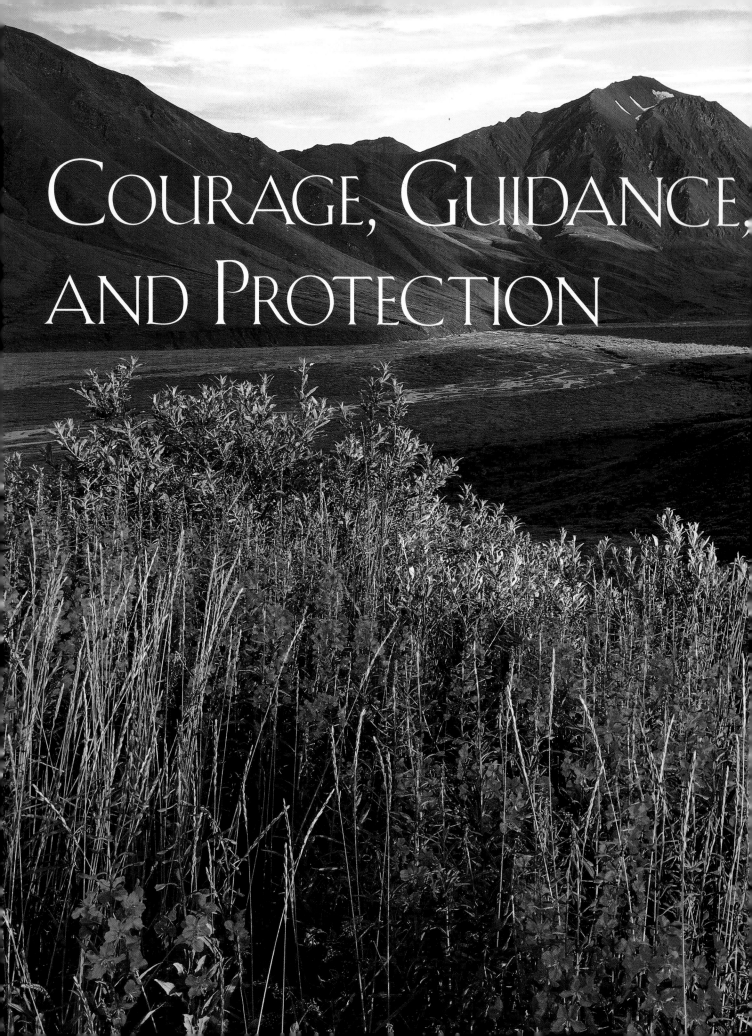

COURAGE, GUIDANCE, AND PROTECTION

CHAPTER FIVE

And lead us not into temptation, but deliver us from evil . . .

Praying for Guidance

ROBERT SCHULLER

The walk of faith is an adventure in a holy partnership. You are a human being with a mortal starting point at birth and a mortal terminal point at death. The span between your birth and death is your earthly life. Your purpose is to fit into a holy scheme and become a participant with God. He created the world and all of us human beings for the purpose of creatively achieving His holy and happy purposes.

You are walking the walk of faith when you dream God's dreams and seek God's guidance.

Therefore, faith is not merely a super-aggressive activity into which you plunge with a gung-ho attitude, to achieve the first impulse that explodes in your mind. Rather, faith is a steady, stable, and steadfast process of opening your conscious and subconscious mind through prayer to the Holy Spirit. The eternal God will shape your will and direct your way!

God promised He will give you guidance.

In the depth of your heart, you know with an unflinching certainty, and with an invincible awareness, the course of action your life must take. This is God Himself, answering your prayers for guidance. He gives you a strong and powerful will to proceed along the determined pathway. Consider these prayers of affirmation:

I am driven by a divine destiny.

I am praying for guidance now.

I am opening my mind consistently and constantly to God, the way the tip of a branch is unceasingly alert and responsive to the wind!

Shew me thy ways, O Lord; teach me thy paths. Lead me in thy truth and teach me: for thou art the God of my salvation .

PSALM 25:4–5

Prayer for Courage

AUTHOR UNKNOWN

O Thou, the Captain of my salvation, strengthen me inwardly and outwardly that I may be vigorous with spiritual purpose and disposed to every virtuous and gallant undertaking. Grant that I may do valiantly despite slothfulness or timidity, and that neither my fear of ridicule nor my love of popularity may make me seem to like what is not right. Be Thou pleased also to fortify my spirit so that I may meet life hopefully and be able to endure everything which Thou mayest be pleased to send me.

Courage to Live

To those who have tried and seemingly have failed,
Reach out, dear Lord, and comfort them today;
For those whose hope has dimmed, whose faith has paled,
Lift up some lighted heavenly torch, I pray.

They are so frightened, Lord, reach out a hand.
They are so hurt and helpless; be their friend.
Baffled and blind, they do not understand—
They think this dark and tangled road the end.

Oh, touch to flame their hope that has burned low,
And strike with fire faith's ashes that are dead.
Let them walk proudly once again, and go
Seeking the sure and steadfast light ahead.

Help them to move among their fellow men
With courage to live, courage to try again.
GRACE NOLL CROWELL

*In all thy ways acknowledge him,
and he shall direct thy paths.*

PROVERBS 3:6

*Whom have I in heaven but thee?
and there is none upon earth that I
desire beside thee. My flesh and my
heart faileth: but God is the strength
of my heart, and my portion for ever.*

PSALM 73:25–26

The Twentieth Psalm

The Lord give ear to thee in thy distress
And be thy shield when troubles thee oppress,
And let His help come down from heaven for thee,
And strength from Sion hill imparted be;

Let Him remember and accept withal
Thine offerings and thy sacrifices all,
And of His bounty evermore fulfill
Thy heart's desire and satisfy thy will.

But we will glory in our great God's name
And joy in our salvation through the same,
And pray unto the Lord our God that He
The effect of all thy prayers will grant to thee.

He now I know will hear and help will bring,
With His strong hand to His anointed king;
On chariots some, on horses some rely,
But we invoke the name of God most high.

Those others are bowed down and fall full low,
When we are risen and upright do go;
Save us, O Lord of heaven, and hear us thence,
When we invoke Thy name for our defense.
JOHN DAVIES

THE LORD HEAR THEE IN THE DAY OF TROUBLE

The LORD hear thee in the day of trouble;
    the name of the God of Jacob defend thee;
Send thee help from the sanctuary,
    and strengthen thee out of Zion;
Remember all thy offerings,
    and accept thy burnt sacrifice;
    Selah.
Grant thee according to thine own heart,
    and fulfill all thy counsel.
We will rejoice in thy salvation,
    and in the name of our God

we will set up our banners:
    the LORD fulfill all thy petitions.
Now know I that the LORD saveth his anointed;
    he will hear him from his holy heaven
    with the saving strength of his right hand.
Some trust in chariots, and some in horses:
    but we will remember the name of the LORD our God.
They are brought down and fallen:
    but we are risen, and stand upright.
Save, LORD: let the king hear us when we call.

PSALM 20

AND LEAD US NOT INTO TEMPTATION, BUT DELIVER US FROM EVIL

LONG IS THE WAY

Long is the way, and very steep the slope,
Strengthen me once again, O God of Hope.

Far, very far, the summit doth appear;
But Thou art near my God, but Thou art near.

And Thou wilt give me with my daily food,
Powers of endurance, courage, fortitude.

Thy way is perfect; only let that way
Be clear before my feet from day to day.

Thou art my Portion, saith my soul to Thee,
O what a Portion is my God to me.
AMY CARMICHAEL

When thou liest down,
thou shalt not be afraid: yea,
thou shalt lie down, and thy
sleep shall be sweet. For the
LORD shall be thy confidence,
and shall keep thy foot from
being taken.
PROVERBS 3:24, 26

GIVE US STRENGTH

Give us strength to do Your will.
Do not dwell on the sins we have committed
Or on the sins we shall commit.
Put out of Your mind our many failings.

Keep no record of our wrongs,
Both those which were deliberate
And those which we could not help.
Remember, Lord, that men are apt to slip,
That we are a weak and spineless race,
Apt to blunder and fall.
Our skins may seem clear and fresh,
But beneath the surface are festering spiritual sores.

O God, we know You are well disposed to us,
So give us Your strength and support.
Help us to live by the precepts of our faith;
Fill our minds with the light of Your love.
We have heard the holy teachings of Your Son.

Let us not be content merely to hear Him,
But give us the desire to obey Him.
Teach us always to look upwards,
Seeking to probe with our prayers the mystery of heaven.
May the vision of Your heavenly kingdom
Guide our actions on earth. Amen.
AUTHOR UNKNOWN

PRAYER OF COURAGE
THE SCOTTISH BOOK OF COMMON PRAYER

O Lord God, our heavenly Father, regard, we beseech Thee, with Thy divinity, the pains of all Thy children; and grant that the passion of our Lord and His infinite merits may make fruitful for good the miseries of the innocent, the sufferings of the sick, and the sorrow of the bereaved; through Him who suffered in our flesh and died for our sake, Thy Son, our Saviour Jesus Christ.

Courage to Seek God

Peter Marshall

It is good, O Lord, that it is not custom that brings us again into this sacred moment of prayer, but our deep sense of need. Forgive us all that we talk too much and think too little. Forgive us all that we worry so often and pray so seldom.

Most of all, O Lord, forgive us that, so helpless without Thee, we are yet so unwilling to seek Thy help. Give us grace to seek Thee with the whole heart.

The LORD will give strength unto his people; the LORD will bless his people with peace.

PSALM 29:11

117

AND LEAD US NOT INTO TEMPTATION, BUT DELIVER US FROM EVIL

On Milton's Blindness

When I consider how my light is spent,
    Ere half my days, in this dark world and wide,
    And that one talent which is death to hide
    Lodged with me useless, though my soul more bent
To serve therewith my Maker, and present
    My true account, lest he returning chide,
    "Doth God exact day-labour, light denied?"
    I fondly ask. But Patience, to prevent
That murmur, soon replies: "God doth not need
    Either man's work or his own gifts; who best
    Bear his mild yoke, they serve him best. His state
Is Kingly: thousands at his bidding speed,
    And post o'er land and ocean without rest;
    They also serve who only stand and wait."

JOHN MILTON

Prayer for Those Who Suffer

SAINT AUGUSTINE

Watch Thou, dear Lord, with those who wake or watch or weep tonight, and give Thine angels charge over those who sleep.

Tend Thy sick ones, O Lord Christ; rest Thy weary ones; bless Thy dying ones; soothe Thy suffering ones; shield Thy joyous ones; and all for Thy love's sake.

Prayer for Divine Teaching

JOHN HENRY NEWMAN

O my Lord, I need Thee to teach me day by day, according to each day's opportunities and needs. Give me that purity of conscience which alone can receive inspirations. My ears are dull so that I cannot hear Thy voice. My eyes are dim so that I cannot see Thy tokens. Thou alone canst quicken my hearing and purge my sight and renew my heart. Teach me to sit at Thy feet and to hear Thy word. Amen.

Prayer for Grace to Forbear

Robert Louis Stevenson

Our Father, purge out of every heart the lurking grudge; give us grace and strength to forbear and to persevere. Give us grace to accept and to forgive offenses. Forgetful ourselves, help us to bear cheerfully the forgetfulness of others. Give us courage, gaiety, and the quiet mind. Spare to us our friends, soften to us our enemies. Bless us, if it may be, in all our innocent endeavors. Give us the strength to encounter that which is to come, that we be brave in peril, constant in tribulation, temperate in wrath, and in all changes of fortune and down to the gates of death, loyal and loving one to another; for Christ's sake. Amen.

Prayer for Strength

Robert Louis Stevenson

We beseech Thee, Lord, to behold us with favor, folk of many families and nations gathered together in peace of this roof, weak men and women existing under the cover of Thy patience.

Be patient still; suffer us yet a little longer—with our broken purposes of good, with our idle endeavors against evil; suffer us awhile longer to endure, and (if it may be) help us to do better.

Bless to us our extraordinary mercies; if the day come when these must be taken, brace us to play the man under affliction.

Prayer for Courage

L. Clark Seelye

Almighty and eternal God, give unto us courage and faith and hope and love that we, in our day and generation, may do all that Thou requirest of us with an eye single to Thine honor and Thy glory.

May we never be discouraged or disheartened because the right seems to fail and the wrong seems to prevail, assured that Thou wilt cause all things at last to work together, so that Thy kingdom of peace and righteousness may prevail throughout all the earth. We beseech Thee to have mercy on us in all our iniquities, Thou just and righteous one. Overcome the strife of opposing foes. Help us to bear one another's burdens and so fulfill Thy law.

Follow Me

The next day John seeth Jesus coming unto him,
  and saith, Behold the Lamb of God,
    which taketh away the sin of the world.
Again the next day after John stood,
  and two of his disciples;
And looking upon Jesus as he walked, he saith,
  Behold the Lamb of God!
And the two disciples heard him speak,
  and they followed Jesus.
The day following Jesus would go forth into Galilee,
  and findeth Phillip, and saith unto him, Follow me.

JOHN 1:29, 35–37, 43

Simply wait upon Him. So doing,
we shall be directed, supplied,
protected, corrected, and rewarded.

VANCE HAVNER

A Prayer for Right Living

I asked for strength that I might achieve;
  I was made weak that I might learn humbly to obey.
I asked for health that I might do great things;
  I was given infirmity that I might do better things.
I asked for riches that I might be happy;
  I was given poverty that I might be wise.
I asked for power that I might have the praise of men;
  I was given weakness that I might feel the need of God.
I asked for all things that I might enjoy life;
  I was given life that I might enjoy all things.
I got nothing that I had asked for, but everything that I had hoped for.
  Almost despite myself, my unspoken prayers were answered;
I am among all men, most richly blessed.

UNKNOWN CONFEDERATE SOLDIER

Open Thou Mine Eyes

Open Thou mine eyes and I shall see;
Incline my heart and I shall desire;
Order my steps and I shall walk
In the ways of Thy commandments.

O Lord God, be Thou to me a God;
And beside Thee let there be none else,
No other, nought else with Thee.

Vouchsafe to me to worship Thee and serve Thee
According to Thy commandments,
  In truth of spirit,
  In reverence of body,
  In blessing of lips,
  In private and public.
Amen.

LANCELOT ANDREWES

A Prayer for Guidance

Lord, I am blind and helpless,
Stupid and ignorant.
Cause me to hear;
Cause me to know;
Teach me to do;
Lead me.

HENRY MARTYN

LEAD US, GOOD SHEPHERD

Father Almighty, bless us with Thy blessing;
    Answer in love Thy children's supplication;
Hear Thou our prayer, the spoken and unspoken;
    Hear us, our Father.

Shepherd of souls, who bringest all who seek Thee
    To pastures green beside the peaceful waters,
Tenderest guide in ways of cheerful duty,
    Lead us, good Shepherd.

Father of mercy, from Thy watch and keeping
    No place can part, nor hour of time remove us;
Give us Thy good, and save us from our evil,
    Infinite Spirit!
BERWICK HYMNAL

LORD OF THE LOVING HEART

Lord of the loving heart,
May mine be loving too.
Lord of the gentle hands,
May mine be gentle too.
Lord of the willing feet,
May mine be willing too.
So may I grow more like Thee
In all I say and do.
AUTHOR UNKNOWN

121

A Prayer

My Lord, I pray that through today
I may walk patiently,
Forgetting not that Thy dear hand
Is leading me.

I know not what Thy wisdom, Lord,
May choose for me today;
What the long hours may hold for me
I cannot say.

I only know that I may go
Unquestioningly with Thee,
Remembering that what Thou wilt
Is best for me.

For Thou, O Lord, canst see the end,
While I but see the way;
Help me to walk it patiently
Throughout today.

Grace Noll Crowell

Prayer for Patience

Thomas Fuller

Lord, teach me the art of patience whilst I am well, and give me the use of it when I am sick. In that day either lighten my burden or strengthen my back. Make me, who so often in my health have discovered my weakness presuming on my own strength, to be strong in my sickness when I solely rely on Thy assistance. Amen.

Prayer for Inner Strength

I know somehow that time will heal this sorrow,
This bitter grief, and that the years will bring
Forgetfulness and peace, that some tomorrow
Will hold no memory of my suffering.
And I believe that there will be a blurring
Of the jagged edges of the wounds I bear,
And in my heart again will be the stirring
Of laughter that has long been absent there.

I know all this, yet still cannot remember;
I cannot see beyond this wall of tears.
Yet as the falling ashes cool an ember,
So will my heart find comfort through the years.
I know—but God, dear God, my need is great!
Give me the inner strength this day to wait.

Grace Noll Crowell

A Prayer

May the strength of God pilot us.
May the power of God preserve us.
May the wisdom of God instruct us.
May the hand of God protect us.
May the way of God direct us.
May the shield of God defend us.

Patrick of Ireland

Jesus, Lead the Way

Jesus, lead the way
Through our life's long day;
When at times the way is cheerless,
Help us follow, calm and fearless;
Guide us by Your hand
To the promised land.

Jesus be our light,
In the midst of night;
Let not faithless fear o'ertake us;
Let not faith and hope forsake us;
May we feel You near
As we worship here.

When in deepest grief,
Strengthen our belief;
When temptations come alluring,
Make us patient and enduring;
Lord, we seek Your grace
In this holy place.

Jesus, still lead on,
Til our rest be won;
If You lead us through rough places,
Grant us Your redeeming graces.
When our course is o'er,
Open heaven's door.

Nicholas L. von Zinzendorf

AND LEAD US NOT INTO TEMPTATION, BUT DELIVER US FROM EVIL

Fix our steps, O Lord, that we may not stagger at the uneven motions of the world, but steadily go on to our glorious home, neither censuring our journey by the weather we meet with, nor turning out of the way by anything that befalls us . . . through Jesus Christ our Lord. Amen.

JOHN WESLEY

PRAYER FOR GUIDANCE

PETER MARSHALL

O God our Father, history and experience have given us so many evidences of Thy guidance to nations and to individuals that we should not doubt Thy power or Thy willingness to direct us. Give us the faith to believe that when God wants us to do or not to do any particular thing, God finds a way of letting us know it.

May we not make it more difficult for Thee to guide us, but be willing to be led of Thee, that Thy will may be done in us and through us for the good of America and all mankind.

This we ask in Jesus' name. Amen.

LEAD, KINDLY LIGHT

Lead, kindly Light, amid the encircling gloom,
    Lead Thou me on;
The night is dark, and I am far from home,
    Lead Thou me on;
Keep Thou my feet. I do not ask to see
The distant scene; one step's enough for me.

I was not ever thus, nor prayed that Thou
    Shouldst lead me on;
I loved to choose and see my path, but now
    Lead Thou me on;

I loved the garish day, and, spite of fears,
Pride ruled my will. Remember not past years.

So long Thy power hath blessed me; sure it still
    Will lead me on
O'er moor and fen, o'er crag and torrent, till
    The night is gone;
And with the morn those angel faces smile,
Which I have loved long since and lost awhile.

JOHN HENRY NEWMAN

Lead Us, O Father

Lead us, O Father, in the paths of peace;
  Without Thy guiding hand we go astray,
And doubts appall, and sorrows still increase;
  Lead us through Christ, the true and living Way.

Lead us, O Father, in the paths of truth;
  Unhelped by Thee, in error's maze we grope,
While passion stains, and folly dims our youth,
  And age comes on, uncheered by faith and hope.

Lead us, O Father, in the paths of right;
  Blindly we stumble when we walk alone,
Involved in shadows of a darksome night;
  Only with Thee we journey safely on.

Lead us, O Father, to Thy heavenly rest,
  However rough and steep the path may be,
Through joy or sorrow, as Thou deemest best,
  Until our lives are perfected in Thee.

WILLIAM H. BURLEIGH

AND LEAD US NOT INTO TEMPTATION, BUT DELIVER US FROM EVIL   GUIDANCE

THE LORD IS MY SHEPHERD

*O Thou, my God, stand by me,
against all the world.*
MARTIN LUTHER

*The Lord my pasture shall prepare,
And feed me with a shepherd's care;
His presence shall my wants supply,
And guard me with a watchful eye.*
JOSEPH ADDISON

The LORD is my shepherd; I shall not want.
He maketh me to lie down in green pastures:
    he leadeth me beside the still waters.
He restoreth my soul: he leadeth me
    in the paths of righteousness for his name's sake.
Yea, though I walk through the valley
    of the shadow of death, I will fear no evil:
    for thou art with me; thy rod and thy staff they comfort me.
Thou preparest a table before me in the presence of mine enemies:
    thou anointest my head with oil; my cup runneth over.
Surely goodness and mercy shall follow me all the days of my life:
    and I will dwell in the house of the LORD for ever.
PSALM 23

Prayer is putting oneself under God's influence.

HARRY EMERSON FOSDICK

THE TWENTY-THIRD PSALM

The God of love my shepherd is,
　　And He that doth me feed;
While He is mine and I am His,
　　What can I want or need?

He leads me to the tender grass,
　　Where I both feed and rest;
Then to the streams that gently pass:
　　In both I have the best.

Or if I stray, He doth convert
　　And bring my mind in frame;
And all this not for my desert,
　　But for His holy name.

Yea, in death's shady black abode
　　Well may I walk, not fear.
For Thou art with me and Thy rod
　　To guide, Thy staff to bear.

Nay, Thou dost make me sit and dine,
　　Even in my enemies' sight;
My head with oil, my cup with wine
　　Runs over day and night.

Surely Thy sweet and wondrous love
　　Shall measure all my days;
And as it never shall remove,
　　So neither shall my praise.

GEORGE HERBERT

AND LEAD US NOT INTO TEMPTATION, BUT DELIVER US FROM EVIL

*If your knees are shaking,
kneel on them.*

CHARLES L. ALLEN

Prayer for Preservation

Author Unknown

O God, let me not turn coward before the difficulties of the day or prove recreant to its duties. Let me not lose faith in my fellow men. Keep me sweet and sound of heart, in spite of ingratitude, treachery, or meanness. Preserve me from minding little stings or giving them. Amen.

The King of Love My Shepherd Is

The King of love my shepherd is,
    Whose goodness fails me never;
I nothing lack if I am His,
    And He is mine for ever.

Where streams of living water flow
    My ransomed soul He's leading;
And where the verdant pastures grow
    With food celestial feeding.

Confused and foolish oft I strayed,
    But yet in love He sought me;
And on His shoulder gently laid,
    And home, rejoicing, brought me.

In death's dark vale I fear no ill
    With You, dear Lord, beside me;
Your rod and staff my comfort still,
    Your cross before to guide me.

You spread a table in my sight,
    Your saving grace bestowing;
And, oh, what transport of delight
    From Your pure chalice flowing!

And so through all the length of days,
    Your goodness fails me never;
Good Shepherd, may I sing Your praise
    Within Your house forever.

Henry W. Baker

My Shepherd Will Supply My Need

My Shepherd will supply my need,
    The God of love supreme;
In pastures green You make me feed,
    Beside the living stream.

You bring my wand'ring spirit back,
    When I forsake Your ways;
And lead me for Your mercy's sake,
    In paths of truth and grace.

When I walk through the shades of death,
    Your presence is my stay;
One word of Your supporting breath
    Drives all my fears away.

Your hand, in sight of all my foes,
    Does still my table spread;
My cup with blessings overflows;
    Your oil anoints my head.

The sure provisions of my God
    Attend me all my days;
Oh, may Your house be my abode,
    And all my work be praise!

There would I find a settled rest,
    While others go and come;
No more a stranger nor a guest,
    But like a child at home.

Isaac Watts

Prayer for Protection

MARTIN LUTHER

My Heavenly Father, I thank You through Jesus Christ, Your beloved Son, that You have protected me by Your grace. Forgive, I pray, all my sins and the evil I have done. Protect me by Your grace tonight. I put myself in your care, body and soul and all that I have. Let Your holy angels be with me, so that the evil enemy will not gain power over me. Amen.

Prayer of Hope

LANCELOT ANDREWES

We beseech Thee, O Lord, remember all for good; have mercy upon all, O God. Remember every soul who, being in any trouble, stands in need of Thy mercy and help: all who are in need or distress, all who love or hate us.

Thou, O Lord, art the Helper of the helpless, the Hope of the hopeless, the Saviour of them who are tossed with tempests, the Haven of them who sail. Be Thou All to all: prosper Thou the work of our hands upon us, prosper Thou our handy-work.

Lord, be Thou within me to strengthen me;
> Without me, to keep me;
> Above me, to protect me;
> Beneath me, to uphold me;
> Before me, to direct me;
> Behind me, to keep me from straying;
> Round about me, to defend me.

Blessed be Thou, O Lord, our Father, forever and ever. Amen.

Prayer before Battle

NICHOLAS RIDLEY

O Heavenly Father, the Father of all wisdom, understanding, and true strength, I beg You, look mercifully on me and send Your Holy Spirit into my breast, that when I must join to fight in the field for the glory of Your Holy Name, then I, being strengthened with the defense of Your right hand, may stand in the confession of Your faith and of Your truth, and continue in the same to the end of my life, through our Lord Jesus Christ.

THE ONLY HOPE OF THE WORLD

O God, that art the only hope of the world,
The only refuge for unhappy men,
Abiding in the faithfulness of heaven,
Give me strong succour in this testing place.

O King, protect Thy man from utter ruin
Lest the weak faith surrender to the tyrant,
Facing innumerable blows alone.
Remember I am dust and wind and shadow,
And life as fleeting as the flower of grass.
But may the eternal mercy which hath shone
From time of old,
Rescue Thy servant from the jaws of the lion.

Thou who didst come from on high in the cloak of flesh,
Strike down the dragon with that two-edged sword,
Whereby our mortal flesh can war with the winds
And beat down strongholds with our Captain God.
Amen.
BEDE

JESUS, MY LORD

Jesus, my Lord,
Come to me;
Comfort me; console me.
Visit the hearts
In strange lands
Yearning for You.
Visit the dying and those
Who are dying without You.

Jesus, my Lord,
Visit also those
Who persecute You.
Lord Jesus, You are my light
In the darkness.
You are my warmth
In the cold.
You are my happiness
In sorrow.
AUTHOR UNKNOWN

CLOTHER OF THE LILY

Protect me, my Lord; my boat is so small, and Your ocean so big.

BRETON FISHERMAN'S PRAYER

Clother of the lily, Feeder of the sparrow,
Father of the fatherless, dear Lord,
Tho' Thou set me as a mark against Thine arrow,
As a prey unto Thy sword,
As a ploughed-up field beneath Thy harrow,
As a captive in Thy cord,
Let that cord be love; and some day make my narrow
Hallowed bed according to Thy Word. Amen.

CHRISTINA ROSSETTI

Prayer for Those
Who Are Misjudged

Christina Rossetti

O Lord, strengthen and support, we entreat Thee, all persons unjustly accused or underrated. Comfort them by the ever-present thought that Thou knowest the whole truth and wilt, in Thine own good time, make their righteousness as clear as the light. Give them grace to pray for such as do them wrong, and hear and bless them when they pray; for the sake of Jesus Christ our Lord and Saviour. Amen.

But I say unto you, Love your enemies, bless them that curse you, do good to them that hate you, and pray for them which despitefully use you, and persecute you.

Matthew 5:44

Prayer for Protection

Christina Rossetti

O Lord, who art as the shadow of a great rock in a weary land, who beholdest Thy weak creatures, weary of labor, weary of pleasure, weary of hope deferred, weary of self. In Thine abundant compassion and unutterable tenderness, bring us, we pray Thee, unto Thy rest. Amen.

Prayer for Steadfastness
and Understanding

Thomas Aquinas

Give me, O Lord, a steadfast heart, which no unworthy affection may drag downwards; give me an unconquered heart, which no tribulation can wear out; give me an upright heart, which no unworthy purpose may tempt aside.

Bestow upon me also, O Lord my God, understanding to know Thee, diligence to seek Thee, wisdom to find Thee, and a faithfulness that may finally embrace Thee. Amen.

HOPE, JOY, AND PEACE

CHAPTER SIX

For thine is the kingdom, and the power, and the glory, for ever . . .

THE INSTINCT OF PRAYER

LAURENCE STERNE

Sure never exhortation to prayer and worship can be better enforced than upon this principle: that God is the cause and creator of all things; that each individual being is upheld in the station it was first placed, by the same hand which first formed it; that all the blessings and advantages which are necessary to the happiness and welfare of beings on earth are only to be derived from the same fountain and that the only way to do it is to secure an interest in His favour, by a grateful expression of our sense for the benefits we have received, and a humble dependence upon Him for those we expect and stand in want of.

Of all duties, prayer certainly is the sweetest and most easy. There are some duties which may seem to occasion a troublesome opposition to the natural workings of flesh and blood, such as the forgiveness of injuries and the love of our enemies, but this duty of prayer and thanksgiving to God, it requireth no strength of parts or painful study, but just to know and have a true sense of our dependence and of the mercies by which we are upheld. And with this, in every place and posture of the body, a good man may lift up his soul unto the Lord his God. For it seems to be the least that can be done to answer the demand of our duty in this point, successively to open and shut up the day in prayer and thanksgiving; since there is not a morning thou risest or a night thou layest down, but thou art indebted for it to the watchful providence of Almighty God.

Every good and perfect gift is from above, and cometh down from the Father of lights, with whom is no variableness, neither shadow of turning.

JAMES 1:17

Happy is he that hath the God of Jacob for his help, whose hope is in the LORD his God: Which made heaven, and earth, the sea, and all that therein is.

PSALM 146:5–6

Tell God all that is in your heart, as one unloads one's heart to a dear friend. People who have no secrets from each other never want subjects of conversations; they do not weigh their words because there is nothing to be kept back.

FRANCOIS FENELON

The wish to pray is a prayer in itself.

GEORGE BERNANOS

THE FORTY-SECOND PSALM

Like as the hart desires the brook
    In summer heat's extreme degree,
With panting breast and wishful look,
    So longs my soul for Thee!

O God, my spirit is athirst
    For God in whom we live and move;
When in God's church shall I be first
    My piety to prove?

My tears have been my constant food,
    Which day and night my griefs supply;
While with malevolence renewed
    "Where is thy God?" they cry.

Now when I think thereon I shed
    By stealth the showers of inward care;
For I before was wont to head
    These multitudes to prayer.

All in one voice of that delight
    Which from the great thanksgiving flows,
As youths and maids, a goodly sight,
    The festive wreath compose.

Why do I drag this loathsome load,
    Whence, O my soul, art thou oppressed;
And what are these the stings that goad
    And wound my tortured breast?

Oh trust in God His power to save
    The cup of thankfulness fulfill,
He keeps thy head above the wave
    And is thy Saviour still.

O God, internal griefs assail;
    I therefore will direct my thought

To Hermon's hill and Jordan's vale,
    Where Thou such wonders wrought.

One sea unto another calls,
    As to the whistling winds they swell;
But at Thy word the tempest falls,
    And I am safe and well.

The Lord is good and loving-kind
    Through all the service of the day,
And Him which made me man and mind
    By night I sing and pray.

I will inquire of God my strength:
    Why hast Thou left me thus to go
With such a load and such a length
    Of life in war and woe?

My bones are smitten to the quick
    As with the falchion's keener blade,
While at my face the cowards kick
    And my distress upbraid.

To wit while reprobates intrude
    My soul's deliverer to deny,
And with malevolence renewed
    "Where is thy God?" they cry.

Why do I drag this loathsome load,
    Whence, O my soul, art thou oppressed;
And what are these the stings that goad
    And wound my tortured breast?

Oh put thy trust in God again
    The cup of thankfulness fulfill;
He shall thy countenance sustain
    And is thy Saviour still.

CHRISTOPHER SMART

O God, Our Help in Ages Past

O God, our help in ages past,
Our hope for years to come,
Our shelter from the stormy blast,
And our eternal home.

Under the shadow of Your throne
Your saints have dwelt secure;
Sufficient is Your arm alone,
And our defense is sure.

Before the hills in order stood
Or earth received its frame,
From everlasting You are God,
To endless years the same.

A thousand ages in Your sight
Are like an evening gone,
Short as the watch that ends the night
Before the rising sun.

Time, like an ever-rolling stream,
Soon bears us all away;
We fly forgotten, as a dream
Dies at the op'ning day.

O God, our help in ages past,
Our hope for years to come,
Still be our guard while troubles last,
And our eternal home.
ISAAC WATTS

A Mighty Fortress Is Our God

A mighty fortress is our God,
A bulwark never failing;
Our helper He, amid the flood
Of mortal ills prevailing.
For still our ancient foe
Doth seek to work us woe;
His craft and power are great
And armed with cruel hate;
On earth is not His equal.

Did we in our own strength confide,
Our striving would be losing;
Were not the right Man on our side,
The Man of God's own choosing.
Dost ask who that may be?
Christ Jesus, it is He;
Lord Sabbaoth, His name,
From age to age the same,
And He must win the battle.

And tho' this world with devils filled
Should threaten to undo us,
We will not fear, for God hath willed
His truth to triumph through us.
The Prince of Darkness grim—
We tremble not for him;
His rage we can endure,
For lo, his doom is sure;
One little word shall fell him.

That word above all earthly powers,
No thanks to them abideth;
The Spirit and the gifts are ours
Thro' Him who with us sideth.
Let goods and kindred go,
This mortal life also;
The body they may kill;
God's truth abideth still;
His kingdom is forever.
Amen.
MARTIN LUTHER

O Lord, Be My Hope

William Wilberforce

O Lord, reassure me with your quickening Spirit; without You I can do nothing. Mortify in me all ambition, vanity, vainglory, worldliness, pride, self-ishness, and resistance from God; and fill me with love, peace, and all the fruits of the Spirit.

O Lord, I know not what I am, but to You I flee for refuge. I would surrender myself to You, trusting Your precious promises and against hope believing in hope. You are the same yesterday, today, and forever; and therefore, waiting on the Lord, I trust I shall at length renew my strength.

God Is Our Refuge

God is our refuge and strength,
    a very present help in trouble.
Therefore will not we fear,
    though the earth be removed, and
    though the mountains be carried
    into the midst of the sea;
Though the waters thereof roar and be troubled,
    though the mountains shake
    with the swelling thereof.
Psalm 46:1–3

So the poor hath hope.
Job 5:16

And now abideth faith, hope, charity, these three; but the greatest of these is charity.
1 Corinthians 13:13

Hope deferred maketh the heart sick.
Proverbs 13:12

Stand by Me, O God

Martin Luther

Do you, my God, stand by me against all the world's wisdom and reason. . . . Not mine but Yours is the cause.

I would prefer to have peaceful days and to be out of this turmoil. But Yours, O Lord, is this cause; it is righteous and eternal. Stand by me, You truly Eternal God! In no man do I trust.

Stand by me, O God, in the name of Your dear Son Jesus Christ, who shall be my Defense and Shelter, yes, my Mighty Fortress, through the might and strength of Your Holy Spirit. Amen.

Joyful, Joyful, We Adore Thee

Joyful, joyful, we adore Thee, God of glory, Lord of love;
Hearts unfold like flowers before Thee, opening to the sun above.
Melt the clouds of sin and sadness; drive the dark of doubt away;
Giver of immortal gladness, fill us with the light of day!

All Thy works with joy surround Thee; earth and heaven reflect Thy rays;
Stars and angels sing around Thee, center of unbroken praise.
Field and forest, vale and mountain, flowery meadow, flashing sea,
Singing bird, and flowing fountain call us to rejoice in Thee.

Thou art giving and forgiving, ever blessing, ever blessed,
Wellspring of the joy of living, ocean depth of happy rest!
Thou our Father, Christ our Brother, all who live in love are Thine;
Teach us how to love each other; lift us to the joy divine.

Mortals, join the happy chorus, which the morning stars began;
Father-love is reigning o'er us, brother-love binds man to man.
Ever singing, march we onward, victors in the midst of strife;
Joyful music leads us sunward in the triumph song of life.

Henry van Dyke

My Soul Shall Be Joyful

*For his anger endureth but a
moment; in his favour is life:
weeping may endure for a night,
but joy cometh in the morning.
Thou hast turned for me my
mourning into dancing:
thou hast put off my sackcloth,
and girded me with gladness.*

Psalm 30:5,11

I will greatly rejoice in the Lord,
    my soul shall be joyful in my God;
    for he hath clothed me with the garments of salvation,
    he hath covered me with the robe of righteousness,
    as a bridegroom decketh himself with ornaments,
    and as a bride adorneth herself with her jewels.
For as the earth bringeth forth her bud,
    and as the garden causeth the things
    that are sown in it to spring forth;
    so the Lord God will cause righteousness
    and praise to spring forth before all the nations.

Isaiah 61:10–11

FOR A JOYFUL SENSE
OF OUR BLESSINGS

WILLIAM ELLERY CHANNING

O God, animate us to cheerfulness. May we have a joyful sense of our blessings, learn to look on the bright circumstances of our lot, and maintain a perpetual contentedness under Thy allotments.

Fortify our minds against disappointment and calamity. Preserve us from despondency, from yielding to dejection. Teach us that no evil is intolerable but a guilty conscience, and that nothing can hurt us, if with true loyalty of affection, we keep Thy commandments and take refuge in Thee; through Jesus Christ our Lord. Amen.

143

Sing unto the Lord a New Song

O sing unto the LORD a new song:
    sing unto the LORD, all the earth.
Sing unto the LORD, bless his name;
    show forth his salvation from day to day.
Declare his glory among the heathen,
    his wonders among all people.
For the LORD is great, and greatly to be praised:
    he is to be feared above all gods.
For all the gods of the nations are idols:
    but the LORD made the heavens.
Honour and majesty are before him:
    strength and beauty are in his sanctuary.
Give unto the LORD, O ye kindreds of the people,
    give unto the LORD glory and strength.
Give unto the LORD the glory due unto his name:
    bring an offering, and come into his courts.
O worship the LORD in the beauty of holiness:
    fear before him, all the earth.
Let the heavens rejoice, and let the earth be glad;
    let the sea roar, and the fulness thereof.
Let the field be joyful, and all that is therein:
    then shall all the trees of the wood rejoice.

PSALM 96:1–9,11,12

THE NINETY-SIXTH PSALM

Sing and let the song be new,
Unto Him that never endeth;
Sing all earth and all in you.
Sing to God and bless His name;
Of the help, the health He sendeth,
Day by day new ditties frame.

Make each country know His worth;
Of His acts the wondered story
Paint unto each people forth.
For Jehovah great alone
All the gods, for awe and glory,
Far above doth hold His throne.

For but idols what are they,
Whom besides made earth adoreth?
He the skies in frame did lay;
Grace and honor are His guides.
Majesty His temple storeth;
Might in guard about Him bides.

Kindreds come Jehovah give,
Oh give Jehovah all together,
Force and fame whereso you live;

Give His name the glory fit;
Take your offerings get you thither,
Where He doth enshrined sit.

Go adore Him in the place
Where His pomp is most displayed;
Earth, oh go with quaking pace,
Go proclaim Jehovah King.
Stayless world shall now be stayed;
Righteous doom His rule shall bring.

Starry roof and earthy floor,
Sea and all thy wideness yieldeth,
Now rejoice and leap and roar.
Leafy infants of the wood,
Fields and all that on you feedeth,
Dance, oh dance, at such a good.

For Jehovah cometh lo!
Lo, to reign Jehovah cometh,
Under whom you all shall go.
He the world shall rightly guide,
Truly as a King becometh,
For the people's weal provide.
MARY SIDNEY HERBERT

MEMORIAL

"God of Abraham, God of Isaac, God of Jacob,"
  not of the philosophers and scholars.
Certainty. Certainty. Emotion. Joy. Peace.
God of Jesus Christ.
"My God and your God."
Your God shall be my God.
Forgetting the world and all things,
  except only God.

He can be found only by the ways taught in the
  Gospel.
Greatness of the human soul.
Righteous Father, the world has not known You,
  but I have known You.
Joy, joy, joy, tears of joy.
BLAISE PASCAL

FOR THINE IS THE KINGDOM, AND THE POWER, AND THE GLORY FOR EVER

JOY

My God, I Thank Thee

My God, I thank Thee, who hast made
　The earth so bright,
So full of splendor and of joy,
　Beauty and light;
So many glorious things are here,
　Noble and right.

I thank Thee, too, that Thou hast made
　Joy to abound,
So many gentle thoughts and deeds
　Circling us round,
That in the darkest spot of earth
　Some love is found.

I thank Thee more that all our joy
　Is touched with pain,
That shadows fall on brightest hours,
　That thorns remain,
So that earth's bliss may be our guide,
　And not our chain.

For Thou who knowest, Lord, how soon
　Our weak heart clings,
Hast given us joys, tender and true,
　Yet all with wings,
So that we see gleaming on high
　Dimmer things.

I thank Thee, Lord, that Thou hast kept
　The best in store;
We have enough, yet not too much
　To long for more:
A yearning for a deeper peace
　Not known before.

I thank Thee, Lord, that here our souls,
　Though amply blessed,
Can never find, although they seek
　A perfect rest,
Nor ever shall, until they lean
　On Jesus' breast.

ADELAIDE ANNE PROCTER

PRAYER OF JOY

CHARLES H. SPURGEON

Come and help us, Lord Jesus. A vision of Your face will brighten us but to feel Your Spirit touching us will make us vigorous.

Oh! For the leaping and walking of the man born lame. May we today dance with holy joy like David before the ark of God. May a holy exhilaration take possession of every part of us; may we be glad in the Lord; may our mouth be filled with laughter and our tongue with singing: "For the Lord hath done great things for us whereof we are glad."

THE WONDERFUL WORKS OF YOUR HANDS

How wonderful, O Lord, are the works
    of Your hands!
The heavens declare Your glory;
The arch of sky displays Your handiwork.
In Your love You have given us the power
To behold the beauty of Your world
Robed in all its splendor.

The sun and stars, the valleys and hills,
The rivers and lakes all disclose Your presence.
The roaring breakers of the sea tell
    of Your awesome might;
The beasts of the field and the birds of the air
Bespeak Your wondrous will.

In Your goodness, You have made us able to hear
The music of the world. The voices of loved ones
Reveal to us that You are in our midst.
A divine voice sings through all creation.
AUTHOR UNKNOWN

LET ALL THINGS NOW LIVING

Let all things now living
A song of thanksgiving
To God our Creator triumphantly raise,
Who fashioned and made us,
Protected and stayed us,
By guiding us on to the end of our days.
God's banners are o'er us;
Pure light goes before us,
A pillar of fire shining forth in the night,
Till shadows have vanished and
Darkness is banished,
As forward to travel from light into Light.

His law He enforces;
The stars in their courses
The sun in its orbit obediently shine.
The hills and the mountains,
The rivers and fountains,
The depths of the ocean proclaim God divine.
We, too, should be voicing
Our love and rejoicing;
With glad adoration, a song let us raise,
Till all things now living
Unite in thanksgiving,
To God in the highest, hosanna and praise.
KATHERINE K. DAVIS

FOR THINE IS THE KINGDOM, AND THE POWER, AND THE GLORY FOR EVER

JOY

Prayer for Calming

Søren Kierkegaard

O Lord, calm the waves of this heart; calm its tempests. Calm yourself, O my soul, so that the divine can act in you. Calm yourself, O my soul, so that God is able to repose in you, so that His peace may cover you.

Yes, Father in heaven, often have we found that the world cannot give us peace; oh but make us feel that You are able to give peace. Let us know the truth of Your promise: that the whole world may not be able to take away Your peace.

Prayer for Peace

Thomas Chalmers

So teach us to number our days that we may apply our hearts to wisdom. Lighten, if it be Your will, the pressure of this world's care, and, above all, reconcile us to Your will, and give us a peace which the world cannot take away; through Jesus Christ our Lord. Amen.

The Image of God

O Lord, who seest from yon starry height,
    Centred in one the future and the past,
    Fashioned in Thine own image, see how fast
    The world obscures in me what once was bright!
Eternal Sun, the warmth which Thou hast given
    To cheer life's flowery April, fast decays;
    Yet, in the hoary winter of my days,
    Forever green shall be my trust in heaven.
Celestial King, oh let Thy presence pass
    Before my spirit, and an image fair
    Shall meet that look of mercy from on high,
As the reflected image in a glass
    Doth meet the look of him who seeks it there
    And owes its being to the gazer's eye.

Francisco de Aldana

STILL, STILL WITH THEE

Still, still with Thee, when purple morning breaketh,
    When the bird waketh, and the shadows flee;
Fairer than morning, lovelier than daylight,
    Dawns the sweet consciousness, I am with Thee.

Alone with Thee amid the mystic shadows,
    The solemn hush of nature newly born;
Alone with Thee in breathless adoration,
    In the calm dew and freshness of the morn.

Still, still with Thee, as to each new-born morning
    A fresh and solemn splendor still is given,

So does this blessed consciousness awaking,
    Breathe each day nearness unto Thee and heaven.

When sinks the soul, subdued by toil, to slumber,
    Its closing eyes look up to Thee in prayer;
Sweet the repose beneath Thy wings o'ershading,
    But sweeter still to wake and find Thee there.

So shall it be at last, in that bright morning,
    When the soul waketh and life's shadows flee;
Oh, in that hour, fairer than daylight dawning,
    Shall rise the glorious thought: I am with Thee.

HARRIET BEECHER STOWE

COME, MY WAY, MY TRUTH, MY LIFE

Come, my Way, my Truth, my Life:
Such a Way as gives us breath,
Such a Truth as ends all strife,
Such a Life as killeth death.

Come, my Light, my Feast, my Strength:
Such a Light as shows a feast,
Such a Feast as mends in length,
Such a Strength as makes his guest.

Come, my Joy, my Love, my Heart:
Such a Joy as none can move,
Such a Love as none can part,

Such a Heart as joys in love.

GEORGE HERBERT

TRANQUILLITY

Lord of all tranquillity,
O incline to us Thine ear;
Hide us very privily
When our cruel foe draws near.
Steady Thou the wills that stray,
Purify our penitence,
Move in us that we may pray
And rejoice with reverence.

Fold our souls in silence deep;
Grant us from ourselves to pass;
Lead, Good Shepherd, us Thy sheep
To the fields of tender grass,
Where Thy hush is in the air,
And Thy flowers the hedges dress,
Cause for us to flow forth there
Waters of Thy quietness.

AMY CARMICHAEL

God takes life's pieces and gives us unbroken peace.

W. D. GOUGH

SERENITY PRAYER

REINHOLD NIEBUHR

God grant me the serenity to accept the things I cannot change, courage to change the things I can, and the wisdom to know the difference. Living one day at a time, enjoying one moment at a time, accepting hardship as the pathway to peace. Taking as Jesus did this sinful world as it is, not as I would have it; trusting that He will make all things right if I surrender to His will, that I may be reasonably happy in this life and supremely happy with Him forever in the next.

FOR THINE IS THE KINGDOM, AND THE POWER, AND THE GLORY FOR EVER   PEACE

I Do Not Ask, O Lord

I do not ask, O Lord, that life may be
   A pleasant road;
I do not ask that Thou wouldst take from me
   Aught of its load.

I do not ask that flowers should always spring
   Beneath my feet;
I know too well the poison and the sting
   Of things too sweet.

For one thing, only Lord, dear Lord, I plead:
   Lead me aright,
Though strength should falter and though heart should bleed,
   Through peace to light.

I do not ask, O Lord, that Thou shouldst shed
   Full radiance here;
Give but a ray of peace, that I may tread
   Without a fear.

I do not ask my cross to understand,
   My way to see;
Better in darkness just to feel Thy hand,
   And follow Thee.

Joy is like restless day, but peace divine
   Like quiet night;
Lead me, O Lord, till perfect day shall shine,
   Through peace to light.

ADELAIDE ANNE PROCTER

The Fruits of the Spirit

The fruit of silence is prayer.
The fruit of prayer is faith.
The fruit of faith is love.
The fruit of love is service.
The fruit of service is peace.

MOTHER TERESA

God Be with Me

God be in my head
   and in my understanding;
God be in my eyes
   and in my looking;
God be in my mouth
   and in my speaking;
God be in my heart
   and in my thinking;
God be at my end
   and at my departing.

SARUM PRIMER

O Jesus, Joy of Loving Hearts

O Jesus, joy of loving hearts,
The fount of life and our true light,
We seek the peace Your love imparts
And stand rejoicing in Your sight.

We taste in You our living bread,
And long to feast upon You still;
We drink of You, the fountainhead,
Our thirsting souls to quench and fill.

For You our restless spirits yearn
Where'er our changing lot is cast;
Glad, when Your presence we discern,
Blest, when our faith can hold You fast.

O Jesus, ever with us stay;
Make all our moments calm and bright;
Oh, chase the night of sin away;
Shed o'er the world Your holy Light.

BERNARD OF CLAIRVAUX

In His will is our peace.
DANTE ALIGHIERI

GIVE ME, GOOD LORD

THOMAS MORE

Glorious God, give me grace to amend my life and to have an eye to my end without begrudging death, which to those who die in You, good Lord, is the gate of a wealthy life.

And give me, good Lord, a humble, lowly, quiet, peaceable, patient, charitable, kind, tender, and pitiful mind, in all my works and all my words and all my thoughts, to have a taste of Your holy, blessed Spirit.

Give me, good Lord, a full faith, a firm hope, and a fervent charity, a love of You incomparably above the love of myself.

Give me, good Lord, a longing to be with You, not to avoid the calamities of this world, nor so much to attain the joys of heaven, as simply for love of You.

And give me, good Lord, Your love and favour, which my love of You, however great it might be, could not deserve were it not for Your great goodness.

These things, good Lord, that I pray for, give me Your grace to labour for.

Prayer for Peace

John Henry

O Lord, support us all the day long, until the shadows lengthen and the evening comes, and the busy world is hushed, and the fever of life is over, and our work is done. Then, Lord, in Your mercy grant us a safe lodging and a holy rest and peace at the last through Jesus Christ our Lord. Amen.

For he is our peace.

EPHESIANS 2:14

Our Daily Bread

Give us our daily Bread,
    O God, the bread of strength.
For we have learnt to know
    How weak we are at length.
As children we are weak,
    As children must be fed;
Give us Thy Grace, O Lord,
    To be our daily Bread.

Give us our daily Bread,
    The bitter bread of grief.
We sought earth's poisoned feasts
    For pleasure and relief;
We sought her deadly fruits,
    But now, O God, instead,
We ask Thy healing grief
    To be our daily Bread.

Give us our daily Bread
    To cheer our fainting soul,
The feast of comfort, Lord,
    And peace to make us whole:
For we are sick of tears,
    The useless tears we shed;
Now give us comfort, Lord,
    To be our daily Bread.

ADELAIDE ANNE PROCTER

*God always answers us in the deeps,
never in the shallows of our souls.*

AMY CARMICHAEL

Only a Shadow

The love I have for you, my Lord,
Is only a shadow of Your love for me,
Your deep abiding love.

My own belief in you, my Lord,
Is only a shadow of Your faith in me,
Your deep and trusting faith.

My life is in Your hands.
My love for You will grow, my Lord.
Your light in me will shine.

The dream I have today, my Lord,
Is only a shadow of Your dream for me,
If I but follow You.

The joy I feel today, my Lord,
Is only a shadow of Your joys for me,
Only a shadow of all that will be
When we meet face to face.

MOTHER TERESA

BRING US INTO YOUR HOUSE

JOHN DONNE

Bring us, O Lord God, at the last awakening, into the house and gate of heaven, to enter into that gate and dwell in that house, where there shall be no darkness nor dazzling, but one equal light; no noise nor silence, but one equal music; no fears nor hopes, but an equal possession; no ends nor beginnings, but one equal eternity, in the habitations of Thy majesty and Thy glory, world without end.

HOW AMIABLE ARE THY TABERNACLES

How amiable are thy tabernacles, O LORD of hosts!
My soul longeth, yea, even fainteth for the courts
    of the LORD: my heart and my flesh
    crieth out for the living God.
Yea, the sparrow hath found an house,
    and the swallow a nest for herself,
    where she may lay her young,
    even thine altars, O LORD of hosts,
    my King, and my God.
Blessed are they that dwell in thy house:
    they will be still praising thee.
PSALM 84:1–4

GOD'S LOVE

He prayeth well who loveth well,
    Both man and bird and beast;
He prayeth best who loveth best,
    All things both great and small;
For the dear God who loveth us,
    He made and loveth all.
SAMUEL TAYLOR COLERIDGE

A FINAL PRAYER

I would that thus, when I shall see
The hour of death draw near to me,
Hope, blossoming within my heart,
May look to heaven as I depart.
WILLIAM CULLEN BRYANT

EVENING PRAYER

PETER MARSHALL

Lord Jesus, we come to Thee for an evening blessing; seal within our hearts the inspirations and memories of the day. We ask Thee for the blessing of quietness for every troubled heart, rest for every weary soul, new faith and courage for all who have faced exhausting tasks this day.

We would rest now in Thee and find in this evening hour Thy stillness and Thy peace to bring us into quiet harmony with Thy will.

We give Thee thanks for every challenge that this day has brought, every new vision of God that winged its way across our skies, every whisper of God that we have sensed in the beauty of Thy world, every thought of God that came in quiet moments, every need of Thee that brought us back again to Thee in prayer.

And now, our Father, grant us Thy benediction. Watch over us through the hours of darkness. Refresh us in spirit as well as in body as we sleep. Help us to face the tasks of tomorrow with steady faith and without fear, conscious of Thy presence and Thy guidance, knowing that we are Thine, as we have placed all our trust in Thee. We know that Thou art still able to keep that which we have committed to Thee.

And now may the love of God the Father, the grace of our Lord Jesus Christ, and the fellowship of the Holy Spirit rest upon us all and abide with us now and forevermore. Amen.

But as it is written, Eye hath not seen, nor ear heard, neither have entered into the heart of man, the things which God hath prepared for them that love him.
1 CORINTHIANS 2:9

The grace of the Lord Jesus Christ, and the love of God, and the communion of the Holy Ghost, be with you all. Amen.
2 CORINTHIANS 13:14

PRAYER FOR PEACE

GEORGE FOX

Grant us, O Lord, the blessing of those whose minds are stayed on You, so that we may be kept in perfect peace: a peace which cannot be broken. Let not our minds rest upon any creature, but only in the Creator, not upon goods, things, houses, lands, inventions of vanities, or foolish fashions; lest, our peace being broken, we become cross and brittle and given over to envy. From all such deliver us, O God, and grant us Your peace.

FOR THINE IS THE KINGDOM, AND THE POWER, AND THE GLORY FOR EVER

INDEX

AUTHORS

TITLES

SUBJECTS

PHOTOGRAPHY